Parlez-vous français?

You're about to cross the Channel and you don't speak a word of French? Don't worry about it: this little guide is just what you need.

In the following pages we give the very basics of grammar and pronunciation, just enough to help you understand the structure of the French language. Then, chapter by chapter, we explore the situations you are likely to encounter during your trip; what to say to the people you meet, how to read the menu, how to cope with the telephone, and so on. Each chapter contains a list of phrases and a useful vocabulary to help you make yourself understood. We have kept the phrases as simple as possible; they are not necessarily exact translations, but correspond to the way a French person would say the same thing. The pronunciation is given in square brackets, using the symbols of the International Phonetic Alphabet (IPA) and corresponding to the system that features in most dictionaries. You'll find a handy summary of these symbols on the inside front cover, which you can fold out so it's visible whatever page you are reading.

Contents

Basic Grammar 6

♟ Meeting People 23

Hello, goodbye   24
Who's who   25
About yourself   26
Loves and hates   30
Make a date!   31
People-watching   32

🚗 Getting Around 33

Asking your way   34
In town   36
By taxi   37
By bus and metro   38
By train   39
By plane   40
By boat   41
Car hire   42
On the road   44

🏠 Accommodation 47

Finding a room   48
Checking in   49
At the hotel   50
Camping   53

☕ Dining Out 55

Choosing a restaurant   56
At the restaurant   58
A la carte   60
Bistrot behaviour   70

🛍️ Shopping 71

Shops and boutiques	72
Choosing	73
Fashion	74
At the hairdresser's	78
Photography	80

🎭 Leisure 81

Sightseeing	82
Entertainment	85
Nightlife	86
Sport	88

🧍 Health 89

Consulting a doctor	90
At the pharmacy	94
At the dentist's, at the optician's	96

ℹ️ The Hard Facts 97

Money	98
Communications	100
Weather	104
Public holidays	106
Police	108

◯ Dictionary 109

English-French	110
French-English	125

Fold-out flaps (front and back)

Essential expressions	*i*
French phonetic pronunciation	*ii-iii*
Cardinal numbers	*iv*
Ordinal numbers, Calculations	*v*
Time and date	*vi*

BASIC GRAMMAR

Compared with English, French grammar seems horribly complicated; even the French themselves need reference books to understand all the rules and all the exceptions to them. This chapter gives you the very basics, just enough to help you understand why word endings change, and to encourage you to make up your own sentences on the pattern of those given in the main chapters of the guide. The first battle is learning how to pronounce all those nasal vowels. Once you have mastered that you should know how to say any word you read correctly, as the sound of each group of letters never varies.

Pronunciation

The French and English alphabets have the same number of letters but the sounds are different:

A	[a]		J	[ʒi]		S	[ɛs]
B	[be]		K	[ka]		T	[te]
C	[se]		L	[ɛl]		U	[y]
D	[de]		M	[ɛm]		V	[ve]
E	[e]		N	[ɛn]		W	[dublə ve]
F	[ɛf]		O	[o]		X	[iks]
G	[ʒe]		P	[pe]		Y	[i gʀɛk]
H	[aʃ]		Q	[ky]		Z	[zɛd]
I	[i]		R	[ɛʀ]			

a is slightly lengthened with the addition of a circumflex **â**:

   patte [pat], pâte [pɑt]

e, which is pronounced as in *help* or in *the*, rhymes with *rain* when it has an acute accent (**é**) and *men* when it has a grave accent (**è**):

   miel [mjɛl], semé [səme], sème [sɛm]

A circumflex on an **e** does not necessarily change the pronunciation; generally it indicates that an **s** has disappeared during the centuries of evolution:

   fenêtre (derived from Latin *fenestra*) [fənɛtʀ]

forêt (cf. forest) [fɔʀɛ]

i and **î** are pronounced slightly shorter than **ee** when there is an **e** at the end of the syllable:

fine [fin], vie [vi], abîme [abim]

o can be short as in *hot* or long as in *home*, and is slightly lengthened with a circumflex:

hotte [ɔt], mot [mo], dôme [dom]

u is a sound that does not exist in English. Its a "tighter" version of the **ew** in *chew*. You have to purse up your lips as if you wanted to say **oo**, but you pronounce **ee**; at least, that's what all the books say. It comes with practice.

ou together make **oo**:

foule [ful], poule [pul]

which rhyme with *fool* and *pool*.

eu together make two short **er** sounds, one a bit like the end of *brother*, the other longer, like saying *hurt* with your mouth more open:

feu [fø], seul [sœl]

The four nasal vowels, **an/en**, **in**, **on**, **un** (or **am/em**, **im**, **om**, **um** before **p** and **b**) are pronounced very much as you would say *awng, ang, ong, eung*. However, the **ng** sound is not made in the throat but further forward. Listen to the French when they say:

France [fʀɑ̃s], bien [bjɛ̃], bonjour [bɔ̃zuʀ], un [œ̃]

You should not have any problems with the consonants except **c**, pronounced hard, like **k**, before **a**, **o** and **u**, and sibilant like **s** before **e**, **i** and **y** (in fact, the same rule applies in English). A cedilla (**ç**) cancels the **a**, **o**, **u** rule and makes it sibilant:

carotte [kaʀɔt], ciel [sjɛl], François [fʀɑ̃swa]

s is pronounced as in *sun*, unless it comes between two vowels, when it becomes **z** as in *surprise*:

soleil [sɔlɛj], surprise [syʀpʀiz]

g is hard as in *gone* before **a**, **o** and **u**, and soft like the sound in *pleasure* before **e**, **i** and **y**. Both **g**'s appear in:

garage [gaʀaʒ]

j is always soft as the sound in *pleasure*, and **ch** always soft as in *shall*, never as in church:

joli [ʒɔli], château [ʃɑto]

The **r** comes from behind the tongue and in front of the throat, with the tip of the tongue behind the lower front teeth.

Stress

In French, stress is fairly weak, and it does not have a fixed position in the word. You can say **bon**jour or bon**jour**, or without a stress at all; it all depends on what you want to express. It's best not to worry about it too much and say your words fairly evenly.

Liaison

Consonants at the end of words are often not pronounced, unless the following word in the sentence starts with a vowel or silent **h**, in which case the two words run into each other:

le petit chat [lə pəti ʃa] (the little cat)
les petits chats [le pəti ʃa] (the little cats)
le petit ange [lə pətitãʒ] (the little angel)
les petits anges [le pətizãʒ] (the little angels)
le petit homme [lə pətitɔm] (the little man)
les petits hommes [le pətizɔm] (the little men)
les dix hommes [le dizɔm] (the ten men)

In these last two examples, the final **s** and **x** are pronounced **z**.

A final **d** sounds like a **t**:

le grand homme [lə gʀãtɔm] (the big man)

Nouns

All nouns have a gender – masculine or feminine – and a number – singular or plural. These are indicated by the **definite article** (the):

masculine *le*, feminine *la*, and plural *les*:

le garçon [lə gaʀsɔ̃], *les garçons* [le gaʀsɔ̃] (the boy, the boys)
la fille [la fij], *les filles* [le fij] (the girl, the girls)
le livre [lə livʀ], *les livres* [le livʀ] (the book, the books)
la table [la tabl], *les tables* [le tabl] (the table, the tables)

When the noun begins with a vowel or silent **h**, the vowel in *le* or *la* is replaced by an apostrophe:

l'enfant [lɑ̃fɑ̃], *les enfants* [lezɑ̃fɑ̃] (the child, the children)
l'amour [lamuʀ], *les amours* [lezamuʀ] (love/loves)
l'homme [lɔm], *les hommes* [lezɔm] (man/men)

This is called elision.

Note that some words begin with an "aspirate **h**"; it is silent as usual, but the elision is not made:

le haricot [lə aʀiko] (bean), *la honte* [la ɔ̃t] (shame),
le hibou [lə ibu] (owl)

Many masculine words can be made feminine by adding an **e** (unless there is already one there):

l'ami [lami], *l'amie* [lami] (friend)
le secrétaire [lə səkʀetɛʀ], *la secrétaire* [la sekʀetɛʀ] (secretary)

Sometimes the last consonant is doubled:

le chat [lə ʃa], *la chatte* [la ʃat] (cat)
le chien [lə ʃjɛ̃], *la chienne* [la ʃjɛn] (dog)

But there are lots of exceptions. Words ending in **–er** have the feminine ending **–ère**

le berger [lə bɛʀʒe], *la bergère* [la bɛʀʒɛʀ] (shepherd/ess)

and **–eur** or **–eux** generally become **–euse**:

le menteur [lə mɑ̃tœʀ], *la menteuse* [la mɑ̃tøz] (liar)
l'ambitieux [lɑ̃bisjø], *l'ambitieuse* [lɑ̃bisjøz] (ambitious person)

but *le directeur* [lə diʀɛktœʀ], *la directrice* [la diʀɛktʀis] (director)
le docteur [lə dɔktœʀ], *la doctoresse* [la dɔktɔʀɛs]

As you have just seen, plurals are usually made by adding an **s**, which is not pronounced, except to make a liaison. But again, there are exceptions.

Words ending in **–s**, in **–x** or in **–z** in the singular do not change in the plural:

le mois [lə mwa], *les mois* [le mwa] (month)
le fax [lə faks], *les fax* [le faks] (fax)
le nez [lə ne], *les nez* [le ne] (nose)

The ending **–al** changes to **–aux**:

le cheval [lə ʃəval], *les chevaux* [le ʃəvo] (horse)

except *bal, carnaval, festival, récital* and a few other words which take an **s**).

Most words ending in **–au** or **–eu** take an **x** in the plural:

le cheveu [lə ʃəvø], *les cheveux* [le ʃəvø] (hair)

Words ending in **–ou** take an **s** in the plural:

le clou [lə klu], *les clous* [le klu] (nail)
le trou [lə tʀu], *les trous* [le tʀu] (hole)

except the following seven words which take an **x**:

bijou [biʒu] (jewel), *caillou* [kaju] (pebble),
chou [ʃu] (cabbage), *genou* [ʒənu] (knee), *hibou* [ibu] (owl),
joujou [ʒuʒu] (toy), *pou* [pu] (flea)

When used with the prepositions **à** (to) and **de** (of, from), the definite article is contracted in the masculine and plural forms:

	the	to the	of/from the
masculine singular	*le*	*au*	*du*
feminine singular	*la*	*à la*	*de la*
m/f elided	*l'*	*à l'*	*de l'*
plural	*les*	*aux*	*des*

Je vais au marché (I'm going to the market)
Je reviens du marché (I'm coming back from the market)
Je vais aux puces (I'm going to the flea market)

De also indicates possession:

le château de ma mère (my mother's castle)
la canne de son père (his father's walking stick)
le bruit du moteur (the sound of the engine)

The **indefinite article** (a/an/some) is *un, une, des*:
un garçon, des garçons (a boy, some boys)
une fille, des filles (a girl, some girls)
un livre, des livres (a book, some books)
une table, des tables (a table, some tables)

For nouns that cannot be quantified, use *du, de la, des* for "some":
Prenez du beurre (take some butter)
Mélanger avec de la farine (mix with flour)
Ajouter de l'eau (add some water)
Battre des œufs (beat some eggs)

Adjectives

In French, adjectives are often placed after the noun they qualify:
un écran plat (a flat screen)
un monstre cruel (a cruel monster)
un pull gris (a grey pullover)

However, the adjective has to agree with the gender and number, so for feminine nouns, an **–e** is added:
une assiette plate (a flat plate)
une sorcière cruelle (a cruel witch)
une souris grise (a grey mouse)

and for the plural, an **–s** is added :
des écrans plats	*des assiettes plates*
des monstres cruels	*des sorcières cruelles*
des pulls gris	*des souris grises*

In many cases the adjective can be placed before the noun (in which case *des* becomes *de*):
de plates excuses (feeble excuses)
de belles pommes (beautiful apples)
une grise mine (a grey complexion)
un bon bain chaud (a good hot bath)

As is the case for feminine nouns, there are plenty of exceptions for feminine adjectives. For instance, *beau* (handsome, good-looking) becomes *bel* before a vowel or silent **h** and *belle* in the feminine form:

> *un beau garçon*   *un bel enfant*   *de beaux enfants*
> *une belle fille*   *une belle enfant*   *de belles filles*

Demonstrative Adjectives

The masculine form for "this" (or "that") is *ce* (*cet* before a vowel or a silent **h**); the feminine is *cette*, and the plural for both masculine and feminine is *ces*:

> *ce garçon* (this/that boy), *cet enfant* (this/that child)
> *cette fille* (this/that girl), *ces gens* (these/those people)

If you want to differentiate between this and that (here and there), use the suffixes **-ci** and **-là**:

> *Ce garçon-ci est grand* (this boy is tall)
> *Cette maison-là est belle* (that house is beautiful)
> *Ces gens-là sont drôles* (those people are funny)

N.B. The **demonstrative pronouns** for this and that are *ceci* and *cela*:

> *J'aime ceci, je n'aime pas cela* (I like this, I don't like that)

Possessive Adjectives

These also have to agree in gender and number:

	masculine	feminine	plural
my	*mon*	*ma*	*mes*
your	*ton*	*ta*	*tes*
his/her/its	*son*	*sa*	*ses*
our	*notre*	*notre*	*nos*
your	*votre*	*votre*	*vos*
their	*leur*	*leur*	*leurs*

> *mon chapeau* (my hat), *ta maison* (your house)
> *son ami* (his/her friend), *sa fille* (his/her daughter)
> *leur chat* (their cat), *leurs chiens* (their dogs)

Comparative and Superlative Adjectives

The comparative and superlative forms are formed with:

aussi ... que (as ... as)
plus ... que (more ... than), *le plus* (the most)
moins ... que (less ... than), *le moins* (the least)

For example:

Mon chat est aussi remarquable que le tien
(My cat is as remarkable as yours)
Un chat est plus affectueux qu'une souris
(A cat is more affectionate than a mouse)
Son chat est le plus beau de tous
(His cat is the most handsome of all)
Le film est moins intéressant que le livre
(The film is less interesting than the book)
Ce chapeau est le moins cher de tous
(This hat is the least expensive of all)

The French equivalents of "good, better, best" are *bon, meilleur, le meilleur;* and of "bad, worse, worst" *mauvais, pire, le pire*:

un bon livre, un meilleur livre, le meilleur livre
(a good book, a better book, the best book)
un mauvais exemple, un pire exemple, le pire exemple
(a bad example, a worse example, the worst example)

Adverbs

Adverbs are generally formed by taking the feminine form of the adjective and adding **–ment**:

final, finale, finalement (finally)
heureux, heureuse, heureusement (happily/fortunately)
Heureusement, je n'ai pas raté mon avion
(Fortunately, I didn't miss my plane)

The adverbial form of *bon* is *bien*, of *mauvais*, *mal*, and of *meilleur*, *mieux*:

Tout va bien (All is well)
Il a mal fait ce travail (He did the job badly)
Il va mieux (He's feeling better)

Pronouns

The **personal pronouns**, used as the subject of the verb, are the following:

	unstressed	stressed
I	*je, j'*	*moi*
you	*tu*	*toi*
he, it (masculine)	*il*	*lui*
she, it (feminine)	*elle*	*elle*
we	*nous*	*nous*
you (polite form and plural)	*vous*	*vous*
they (masculine)	*ils*	*eux*
they (feminine)	*elles*	*elles*

Je suis là (I'm here)
Je suis là, moi, mais lui n'est pas encore arrivé.
(I'm here, but he hasn't arrived yet).

Here are the **direct object** and **indirect object** pronouns:

direct object		indirect object	
me	*me (m')*	to me	*me (m')*
you	*te (t')*	to you	*te (t')*
him, it	*le (l')*	to him/it	*lui*
her, it	*la (l')*	to her/it	*lui*
us	*nous*	to us	*nous*
you	*vous*	to you	*vous*
them	les	to them	*leur*

Je le savais (I knew it)
Il les voit (He sees them/He can see them)
Nous l'avons vu (We saw him)
Je lui ai donné un cadeau (I gave him a present)
Elle leur a parlé (She talked to them)

The **possessive pronoun** shows what belongs to whom, and changes
14 depending on the gender and number of the object in question:

	masc. sing.	masc. pl.	fem. sing.	fem. pl.
mine	*le mien*	*les miens*	*la mienne*	*les miennes*
yours	*le tien*	*les tiens*	*la tienne*	*les tiennes*
his, hers, its	*le sien*	*les siens*	*la sienne*	*les siennes*
ours	*le nôtre*	*les nôtres*	*la nôtre*	*les nôtres*
yours	*le vôtre*	*les vôtres*	*la vôtre*	*les vôtres*
theirs	*le leur*	*les leurs*	*la leur*	*les leurs*

> *mon livre, le mien* (my book, mine)
> *ta voiture, la tienne* (your car, yours)
> *ses enfants, les siens* (his children, his)
> *leurs amis, les leurs* (their friends, theirs)

You can also use the "stressed" form of the personal pronoun here:

> *C'est mon livre, donne-le-moi, il est à moi*
> (It's my book, give it to me, it's mine)

The **demonstrative pronouns** are *celui* (m.), *celle* (f), *ceux* (m.pl.)
celles (f.pl.), to which you can add *-ci* or *-là* to point something out:

> *J'hésite entre celui-ci et celui-là*
> (I'm dithering between this one and that one)

The **indefinite pronoun** *on*, equivalent of the English "one", is frequently used in French and can replace any of the personal pronouns, or can represent an indeterminate "they":

> *Qu'est-ce qu'on fait?* (What shall we do?/What are we doing?)
> *On vient!* (Someone's coming!)
> *Ici on parle français* (French is spoken here)
> *On ne sait jamais* (You never know)
> *On a trop mangé hier soir* (We ate too much last night)
> *On danse le flamenco en Espagne*
> (They dance the flamenco in Spain).

It is conjugated the same way as *il* and *elle*, third person singular, but the stressed form is *soi*:

> *On pense toujours à soi* (One always thinks of oneself).

Sometimes it is preceded by *l'* between vowel sounds:

> *Je crois que l'on est en retard* (I think we are late).

Verbs

The main groups of verbs take their name from the ending of the infinitive form, **–er**, **–ir** and **–re**. But first, let's look at the two verbs you will use the most, *être*, to be and *avoir*, to have. These both have irregular conjugations, and you should learn them by heart, as you will need them to conjugate the past tense of all other verbs. Underlined endings are used for all verbs and easy to learn.

Infinitive: *être* (to be) *avoir* (to have)

Present tense			
je suis	I am	*j'ai*	I have
tu es	you are	*tu as*	you have
il/elle est	he/it/she is	*il/elle a*	he/she/it has
nous sommes	we are	*nous avons*	we have
vous êtes	you are	*vous avez*	you have
ils/elles sont	they are	*ils/elles ont*	they have

Imperfect			
j'étais	I was	*j'avais*	I had
tu étais	you were	*tu avais*	you had
il/elle était	he/she/it was	*il/elle avait*	he/she/it had
nous étions	we were	*nous avions*	we had
vous étiez	you were	*vous aviez*	we had
ils/elles étaient	they were	*ils/elles avaient*	they had

Perfect (conjugated with present of *avoir* + past participle *été*)		(present of *avoir* + past participle *eu*)	
j'ai été	I have been	*j'ai eu*	I have had
tu as été	you have been	*tu as eu*	you have had
il/elle a été	he/she/it has been	*il/elle a eu*	he/she/it has had
nous avons été	we have been	*nous avons eu*	we have had
vous avez été	you have been	*vous avez eu*	you have had
ils/elles ont été	they have been	*ils/elles ont eu*	they have had

Future			
Je serai	I shall be	*j'aurai*	I shall have
tu seras	you will be	*tu auras*	you will have
il/elle sera	he/she/it will be	*il/elle aura*	he/she/it will have
nous serons	we shall be	*nous aurons*	we shall have
vous serez	you will be	*vous aurez*	you will have
ils/elles seront	they will be	*ils/elles auront*	they will have

In all verbs, the conditional is formed by taking the future form and adding the same endings as the imperfect tense:

Conditional			
je serais	I would be	*j'aurais*	I would have
tu serais	you would be	*tu aurais*	you would have
il/elle serait	he/she/it would be	*il/elle aurait*	he/she/it would have
nous serions	we would be	*nous aurions*	we would have
vous seriez	you would be	*vous auriez*	you would have
ils/elles seraient	they would be	*ils/elles auraient*	they would have

Verbs with an infinitive ending in **–er**, such as *aimer* (to love), *parler* (to talk), *manger* (to eat) are all conjugated on the pattern shown in the tables below:

Infinitive: *marcher* (to walk), **past participle**: *marché*

Present	Imperfect
je marche	*je marchais*
(I walk, I'm walking)	(I walked, I was walking)
tu marches	*tu marchais*
il/elle marche	*il/elle marchait*
nous marchons	*nous marchions*
vous marchez	*vous marchiez*
ils/elles marchent	*ils/elles marchaient*

Perfect (present of *avoir* + past participle)	**Future** (infinitive+same endings as *être* and *avoir*, future tense)
j'ai marché (I walked, I've walked) *tu as marché* *il/elle a marché* *nous avons marché* *vous avez marché* *ils/elles ont marché*	*je marcherai* (I'll walk) *tu marcheras* *il/elle marchera* *nous marcherons* *vous marcherez* *ils/elles marcheront*

Verbs with an infinitive ending in **–ir**, such as *finir* (to finish), *pâlir* (to grow pale):

Infinitive: *finir* (to finish), **past participle**: *fini*

Present	**Imperfect**
je finis (I finish, I'm finishing) *tu finis* *il/elle finit* *nous finissons* *vous finissez* *ils/elles finissent*	*je finissais* (I finished, I was finishing) *tu finissais* *il/elle finissait* *nous finissions* *vous finissiez* *ils/elles finissaient*

Perfect (present of *avoir* + past participle)	**Future** (infinitive+same endings as *être* future tense)
j'ai fini (I finished, I've finished) *tu as fini* *il/elle a fini* *nous avons fini* *vous avez fini* *ils/elles ont fini*	*je finirai* (I'll finish) *tu finiras* *il/elle finira* *nous finirons* *vous finirez* *ils/elles finiront*

Verbs with an infinitive ending in **–re**: *fondre* (to melt), *rendre* (to give back), *tordre* (to twist):

Infinitive: *perdre* (to lose), **past participle**: *perdu*

Present	Imperfect
je perds (I lose, I'm losing)	*je perdais* (I lost, I was losing)
tu perds	*tu perdais*
il/elle perd	*il/elle perdait*
nous perdons	*nous perdions*
vous perdez	*vous perdiez*
ils/elles perdent	*ils/elles perdaient*

Perfect (present of *avoir* + past participle)	**Future** (infinitive – last e + same endings as *être* and *avoir*, future tense)
j'ai perdu (I lost, I've lost)	*je perdrai* (I'll lose)
tu as perdu	*tu perdras*
il/elle a perdu	*il/elle perdra*
nous avons perdu	*nous perdrons*
vous avez perdu	*vous perdrez*
ils/elles ont perdu	*ils/elles perdront*

The **present participle** is generally formed from the root of the imperfect tense + **–ant**: *étant, marchant, finissant, perdant* (being, walking, finishing, losing). But there is no continuous present in French. To say "I am eating", use the present tense, *je mange*.

Reflexive verbs

These verbs "reflect" the action back onto the subject. The infinitive is always preceded by *se*, for example:

> *se laver* (to get washed, lit. to wash oneself)

Reflexive verbs and those implying movement such as *tomber* (fall), *monter* (climb), *descendre* (go down), *venir* (come), *aller* (go), *partir* (depart), *arriver* (arrive), etc., are conjugated with *être* in the perfect tense, and the past participle has to agree with the subject, masculine, feminine or plural.

Present	Imperfect
Je me lave	*je me lavais*
Tu te laves	*tu te lavais*
Il, elle se lave	*il, elle se lavait*
Nous nous lavons	*nous nous lavions*
Vous vous lavez	*vous vous laviez*
Ils, elles se lavent	*ils se lavaient*

Perfect	Future
je me suis lavé(e)	*je me laverai*
tu t'es lavé(e)	*tu te laveras*
il s'est lavé	*il se lavera*
elle s'est lavée	*elle se lavera*
nous nous sommes lavé(e)s	*nous nous laverons*
vous vous êtes lavé(e)(s)	*vous vous laverez*
ils se sont lavés	*ils se laveront*
elles se sont lavées	*elles se laveront*

Negative form

The most common way of making a positive statement into a negative one is to add *ne … pas* around the verb:

> *Il vient* (He's coming)
> *Il ne vient pas* (He isn't coming)
> *Elle est partie* (She has left)
> *Elle n'est pas partie* (She didn't leave)
> *Je l'ai vu* (I've seen him)
> *Je ne l'ai pas vu* (I haven't seen him)

But there are other negative expressions:

> *ne … personne* (no one)
> *Je ne vois personne* (I can't see anyone)
> *Personne n'est venu* (Nobody came)

ne … plus (no longer)
Il ne vient plus (He isn't coming any more)
ne … jamais (never)
Demain ne vient jamais (Tomorrow never comes)
ne … rien (nothing)
Je n'ai rien fait (I haven't done anything)
ne … que (only)
Je n'ai vu qu'elle (I saw only her)
ne… ni… ni (neither nor)
Je ne sais ni l'heure ni le jour
(I don't know the time nor the day)

Interrogative form

The easy way of asking a question is to change the intonation of the sentence:

Tu l'aimes (You love him)
Tu l'aimes? (Do you love him?)
Tu l'as vu (You saw him)
Tu l'as vu? (Did you see him?)

Otherwise, you can turn the verb around (and put a hyphen between the verb and subject):

L'aimes-tu? (Do you love him?)
L'as-tu vu? (Did you see him?)

Another simple way is to use the expression *Est-ce que…*

Est-ce que tu l'aimes? (Do you love him?)
Est-ce qu'il pleut? (Is it raining?)
Est-ce que tu as vu l'heure? (Have you seen the time?)

The verb is also turned around after interrogative pronouns and adverbs (who, what, why, etc.):

Que (what)

Que vas-tu dire? (What are you going to say?)
Que vois-tu? (What can you see?)
Qu'est-ce qu'il y a? (What's the matter?)

Qui (who, whom)
>*Qui êtes-vous?* (Who are you?)

Quand (when)
>*Quand viendra-t-il?* (When will he come?)

(Note the addition of **-t-** to avoid two clumsy-sounding vowels together.)

Où (where)
>*Où sommes-nous?* (Where are we?)

Pourquoi (why)
>*Pourquoi ment-il?* (Why is he lying?)

Comment (how)
>*Comment es-tu venu?* (How did you come?)

Combien (how much)
>*Combien coûte cette robe?* (How much is this dress?)

A handy little phrase that is often used is *n'est-ce pas?* (literally, "isn't it?"):

>*Tu l'aimes, n'est-ce pas?* (You love him, don't you?)
>*Il vient, n'est-ce pas?* (He's coming, isn't he?)
>*Nous serons cinq, n'est-ce pas?*
>(There'll be five us, won't there?)

You can use it in negative questions, too:

>*Il ne vient pas, n'est-ce pas?* (He isn't coming, is he?)
>*Nous n'y allons pas, n'est-ce pas?*
>(We aren't going there, are we?)
>*Tu ne l'aimes pas vraiment, n'est-ce pas?*
>(You don't really like him, do you?)

If you want to give a contradictory answer to this question, you have to use *si* instead of *oui*:

>*Si, il vient* (Yes, he's coming)
>*Si, nous y allons* (Yes, we are going)
>*Si, je l'adore* (Yes, I adore him)

Meeting People

Don't be shy about talking to people: just smile and say *Bonjour!* The French have a reputation for being grumpy, but you'll soon find out that they don't really bite.

However, your first impressions may well be that people in France are rather reserved and formal. They don't easily get involved in long conversations with strangers. In buses and the metro, on their way to and from work, they tend to sit lost in their thoughts, staring vacantly into space, reading a book or even sleeping. Shopkeepers and waiters may greet you politely but are not likely to ask you where you come from or make comments on the weather. If you want to talk, you'll have to break the ice yourself.

Should you need to ask your way or make some other kind of enquiry, you can attract a person's attention by saying *Excusez-moi, Madame, Mademoiselle* or *Monsieur* as the case may be.

HELLO, GOODBYE

You can greet people with the word *Bonjour* at any time of the day; young people usually say *Salut*, or even the English *Hello*. The French shake hands a lot; among friends, they kiss each other on alternate cheeks (*faire la bise*) two, three or four times depending on the region, when they meet and when they take leave of each other.

Hello (everyone)!	**Bonjour (à tous!)** [bɔ̃ʒuʀ] [a tus]
Good evening, good night	**Bonsoir, bonne nuit** [bɔ̃swaʀ] [bɔn nɥi]
Goodbye	**Au revoir, salut** [o ʀəvwaʀ] [saly]
How do you do?	**Comment allez-vous?** [kɔmãtale vu]
Fine thanks, and you?	**Bien, merci et vous?** [bjɛ̃ mɛʀsi e vu]
What is your name?	**Comment vous appelez-vous?** [kɔmã vuzapəle vu]
My name is...	**Je m'appelle...** [ʒə mapɛl]
I don't speak French very well.	**Je ne parle pas très bien français.** [ʒe nə paʀl pa tʀɛ bjɛ̃ fʀãsɛ]

TU OR VOUS?

There are two ways of saying "you" in French. *Tu* is the familiar form, used for addressing children, close friends and family, and animals. Young people use *tu* among themselves, even the first time they meet. It's a bit like addressing people by their first name in English. *Vous* is more formal, and also the plural of *tu*. When in doubt, play it safe with *vous*. Note that when you say "please" to a friend, *s'il vous plaît* becomes *s'il te plaît*.

Who's who

Maybe you're not travelling alone. Here are some phrases to help you introduce your companions to your new acquaintances.

May I introduce you to Cyril.
Laisse-moi te présenter Cyril.
[lɛs mwa tə prɛzɑ̃te siril]

Come and meet Michelle!
Viens faire la connaissance de Michelle!
[vjɛ̃ fɛr la kɔnɛsɑ̃s də miʃɛl]

Have you met before?
Est-ce que vous vous êtes déjà rencontré(e)s?
[ɛskə vu vuz ɛt deʒa rɑ̃kɔ̃tre]

How do you do. Pleased to meet you.
Enchanté(e)!
[ɑ̃ʃɑ̃te]

These are my parents/ grandparents.
Voici mes parents/ grands-parents.
[vwasi me parɑ̃/grɑ̃parɑ̃]

This is my mother/my father.
Voici ma mère/mon père.
[vwasi ma mɛr/mɔ̃ pɛr]

friend	**mon ami(e)** [mɔnami]	sister	**ma sœur** [ma sœr]
friend *(familiar)*	**mon copain/ ma copine** [mɔ̃ kɔpɛ̃] [ma kɔpin]	brother	**mon frère** [mɔ̃ frɛr]
		family	**ma famille** [ma famij]
boyfriend	**mon petit ami** [mɔ̃ pətitami]	wife	**ma femme** [ma fam]
girlfriend	**ma petite amie** [ma pətitami]	husband	**mon mari** [mɔ̃ mari]
fiancé	**mon fiancé/ ma fiancée** [mɔ̃ fiɑ̃se] [ma fiɑ̃se]	aunt	**ma tante** [ma tɑ̃t]
		uncle	**mon oncle** [mɔ̃nɔ̃kl]
mum	**ma maman** [ma mamɑ̃]	cousin	**mon cousin/ ma cousine** [mɔ̃ kuzɛ̃] [ma kuzin]
dad	**mon papa** [mɔ̃ papa]		

25

ABOUT YOURSELF

Now you'll probably want to tell your new acquaintances something about yourself; where you come from and what you do.

| Where do you come from? | **D'où viens-tu?**
[du vjɛ̃ ty] |
| I come from Great Britain | **Je viens de Grande-Bretagne.**
[ʒə vjɛ̃ də gʀɑ̃d bʀətaɲ] |

England	**d'Angleterre** [dɑ̃glətɛʀ]	Australia	**d'Australie** [dostʀali]
Ireland	**d'Irlande** [diʀlɑ̃d]	New Zealand	**de Nouvelle-Zélande** [də nuvɛl zelɑ̃d]
Scotland	**d'Ecosse** [dekɔs]	USA	**des Etats-Unis** [dez etazyni]
Wales	**du Pays de Galles** [dy pɛj də gal]	Canada	**du Canada** [dy kanada]

| I am... | **Je suis...***
[ʒə sɥi] |

British	**Britannique** [bʀitanik]	Australian	**Australien/ Australienne** [ostʀaljɛ̃] [ostʀaljɛn]
English	**Anglais/ Anglaise** [ɑ̃glɛ] [ɑ̃glɛz]	a New Zealander	**Néo-Zélandais/ Néo-Zélandaise** [neozelɑ̃dɛ] [neozelɑ̃dɛz]
Irish	**Irlandais/ Irlandaise** [iʀlɑ̃dɛ] [iʀlɑ̃dɛz]	American	**Américain/ Américaine** [ameʀikɛ̃] [ameʀikɛn]
Scottish	**Ecossais/ Ecossaise** [ekɔsɛ] [ekɔsɛz]	Canadian	**Canadien/ Canadienne** [kanadjɛ̃] [kanadjɛn]
Welsh	**Gallois/ Galloise** [galwa] [galwaz]		

*Remember that if you are female you will have to use the feminine ending. When we have given alternatives in this guide, the masculine form is given first. When there is no difference in pronunciation, we have simply put "e" in brackets after the masculine, e.g. *marié(e)*.

How old are you?	**Quel âge as-tu?** [kɛl ɑʒ a ty]	
I'm 25.	**J'ai vingt-cinq ans.** [ʒe vɛ̃tsɛ̃kɑ̃]	
When's your birthday?	**Quand as-tu ton anniversaire?** [kɑ̃ a ty tɔnanivɛʀsɛʀ]	
The 4th July.	**Le 4 juillet.** [lə katʀ ʒɥije]	
Are you married?	**Es-tu marié(e)?** [ɛ ty maʀje]	
No, I'm single.	**Non, je suis célibataire.** [nɔ̃ ʒə sɥi selibatɛʀ]	
What do you do for a living?	**Que fais-tu dans la vie?** [kə fɛ ty dɑ̃ la vi]	
I go to work.	**Je travaille.** [ʒə tʀavaj]	
I'm looking for a job.	**Je cherche du travail.** [ʒə ʃɛʀʃ dy tʀavaj]	
I'm out of work.	**Je suis au chômage.** [ʒə sɥiz o ʃomaʒ]	
I'm retired.	**Je suis à la retraite.** [ʒə sɥiz a la ʀətʀɛt]	
I'm a student.	**Je suis étudiant/étudiante.** [ʒə sɥiz etydiɑ̃/etydiɑ̃t]	
What kind of school do you go to?	**Quelle école fréquentes-tu?** [kɛl ekɔl fʀekɑ̃t ty]	
I'm at high school.	**Je suis au lycée.** [ʒə sɥiz o lise]	

college	**à l'école professionnelle** [a lekɔl pʀɔfɛsjɔnɛl]	university	**à l'université** [a lynivɛʀsite]
teacher-training college	**à l'école normale** [a lekɔl nɔʀmal]	faculty of arts/ science	**à la faculté des arts/ des sciences** [a la fakylte dezaʀ] [de sjɑ̃s]

What are you studying?		**Qu'est-ce que tu étudies?** [kɛskə ty etydi]	
I'm studying law		**J'étudie le droit.** [ʒetydi lə dʀwa]	

archaeology	**l'archéologie** [laʀkeɔlɔʒi]	literature	**la littérature** [la liteʀatyʀ]
biology	**la biologie** [la biɔlɔʒi]	mathematics	**les mathématiques** [le matematik]
chemistry	**la chimie** [la ʃimi]	medicine	**la médecine** [la mɛdsin]
computing	**l'informatique** [lɛ̃fɔʀmatik]	philosophy	**la philosophie** [la filɔzɔfi]
economics	**les sciences économiques** [le sjɑ̃s ekɔnɔmik]	physics	**la physique** [la fizik]
geography	**la géographie** [la ʒeogʀafi]	political science	**les sciences po(litiques)** [le sjɑ̃s po]
history	**l'histoire** [listwaʀ]	sociology	**la sociologie** [la sosiɔlɔʒi]
languages	**les langues** [le lɑ̃g]	theology	**la théologie** [la teɔlɔʒi]

What do you want to do when you've finished?		**Que voudrais-tu faire par la suite?** [kə vudʀɛ ty fɛʀ paʀ la sɥit]	
I'd like to be a/an...		**Je voudrais être...** [ʒə vudʀɛz ɛtʀ]	
What's your job?		**Quelle est ta profession?** [kɛl ɛ ta pʀɔfɛsjɔ̃]	
I'm a/an...		**Je suis...** [ʒə sɥi]	

accountant	**comptable** [kɔ̃tabl]	barrister	**avocat/avocate** [avoka] [avokat]
architect	**architecte** [aʀʃitɛkt]	carpenter	**menuisier** [mənɥizje]
artist	**artiste** [aʀtist]	civil servant	**fonctionnaire** [fɔ̃ksjɔnɛʀ]

cook	**cuisinier/ cuisinière** [kɥizinje] [kɥizinjɛʀ]	journalist	**journaliste** [ʒuʀnalist]
		lawyer	**juriste** [ʒyʀist]
craftsman	**artisan** [aʀtizɑ̃]	mechanic	**mécanicien/ mécanicienne** [mekanisjɛ̃] [mekanisjɛn]
director	**directeur/ directrice** [diʀɛktœʀ] [diʀɛktʀis]	model	**mannequin** [manəkɛ̃]
doctor	**médecin** [medsɛ̃]	musician	**musicien/ musicienne** [myzisjɛ̃] [myzisjɛn]
draughtsman	**dessinateur/ dessinatrice** [dɛsinatœʀ] [dɛsinatʀis]	nurse	**infirmier/ infirmière** [ɛ̃fiʀmje] [ɛ̃fiʀmjɛʀ]
driver	**chauffeur** [ʃofœʀ]		
editor	**rédacteur/ rédactrice** [ʀedaktœʀ] [ʀedaktʀis]	office clerk	**employé(e) de bureau** [ɛ̃plwaje də byʀo]
electrician	**électricien/ électricienne** [elɛktʀisjɛ̃] [elɛktʀisjɛn]	painter	**peintre** [pɛ̃tʀ]
		photographer	**photographe** [fɔtɔgʀaf]
engineer	**ingénieur** [ɛ̃ʒenjœʀ]	pilot	**pilote** [pilɔt]
farmer	**agriculteur/ agricultrice** [agʀikyltœʀ] [agʀikyltʀis]	sailor	**marin** [maʀɛ̃]
		secretary	**secrétaire** [səkʀetɛʀ]
firefighter	**pompier** [pɔ̃mpje]	shopkeeper	**commerçant/ commerçante** [kɔmɛʀsɑ̃] [kɔmɛʀsɑ̃t]
gardener	**jardinier/ jardinière** [ʒaʀdinje] [ʒaʀdinjɛʀ]	solicitor	**notaire** [nɔtɛʀ]
hairdresser	**coiffeur/ coiffeuse** [kwafœʀ] [kwaføz]	teacher	**enseignant/ enseignante** [ɑ̃sɛɲɑ̃] [ɑ̃sɛɲɑ̃t]

29

LOVES AND HATES

Whether you like something or love it to bits, you can use the same
verb in French, *aimer*. Its meaning is tempered by the addition of the
adverb *bien*: *je l'aime bien*, I'm fond of him.

I like classical music.	**J'aime la musique classique.** [ʒɛm la myzik klasik]
I like dancing.	**J'aime bien danser.** [ʒɛm bjɛ̃ dãse]
I love my children.	**J'aime mes enfants.** [ʒɛm mez ãfã]
I love chocolate.	**J'adore le chocolat.** [ʒadɔʀ lə ʃɔkɔla]
I don't like modern jazz.	**Je n'aime pas le jazz moderne.** [ʒə nɛm pa lə dʒaz mɔdɛʀn]
I hate singing.	**Je déteste chanter.** [ʒə detɛst ʃãte]
What do you like doing?	**Qu'est ce que tu aimes faire?** [kɛskə ty ɛm fɛʀ]
I like..., but I prefer...	**J'aime bien..., mais je préfère...** [ʒɛm bjɛ̃] [mɛ ʒə pʀefɛʀ]
... reading	**... lire** [liʀ]
... watching TV	**... regarder la télévision** [ʀəgaʀde la televizjɔ̃]
... listening to music	**... écouter de la musique** [ekute də la myzik]
... sport	**... le sport** [lə spɔʀ]
... painting	**... peindre** [pɛ̃dʀ]
... walking in the country	**... me promener à la campagne** [mə pʀɔməne a la kãpaɲ]
... looking round the shops	**... faire les boutiques** [fɛʀ le butik]

MAKE A DATE!

You get on well together? Well, you'd better make sure that at least you swap phone numbers…

Can I see you again?	**Est-ce qu'on peut se revoir?** [ɛskɔ̃ pø sə ʀəvwaʀ]
That would be great!	**Ça serait génial!** [sa səʀɛ ʒenjal]
What would you like to do?	**Qu'est-ce que tu aimerais faire?** [kɛskə ty ɛməʀɛ fɛʀ]
We could…	**Nous pourrions…** [nu puʀiɔ̃]
Is there anything interesting to see?	**Y a-t-il des choses intéressantes à voir?** [jatil de ʃoz ɛ̃teʀesɑ̃t a vwaʀ]
You could show me where you live.	**Tu pourrais me montrer où tu habites.** [ty puʀɛ mə mɔ̃tre u ty abit]
I'd like to take a souvenir home.	**J'aimerais ramener un souvenir du coin.** [jɛməʀɛ ʀaməne œ̃ suvəniʀ dy kwɛ̃]
Are you free on Sunday?	**Es-tu libre dimanche?** [ɛ ty libʀ dimɑ̃ʃ]
What about Monday?	**Que penses-tu de lundi?** [kə pɑ̃s ty də lœ̃di]
What time?	**A quelle heure?** [a kɛl œʀ]
Where?	**Où ça?** [u sa]
What's your phone number?	**Quel est ton numéro de téléphone?** [kɛl ɛ tɔ̃ nymeʀo də telefɔn]
How long are you staying here?	**Combien de temps restes-tu?** [kɔ̃bjɛ̃ də tɑ̃ ʀɛstə ty]

PEOPLE-WATCHING

A few words to help you talk about the people around you, or help you express how you're feeling.

people	**les gens** [lə ʒɑ̃]	young people	**les jeunes** [le ʒœn]
person	**une personne** [yn pɛʀsɔn]	lad	**un mec,** **un gars** [œ̃ mɛk] [œ̃ ga]
baby	**un bébé** [œ̃ bebe]	adult	**un adulte** [œ̃ nadylt]
child	**un enfant** [œ̃ nɑ̃fɑ̃]	man	**un homme** [œ̃ nɔm]
kid	**un gamin** [œ̃ gamɛ̃]	woman	**une femme** [yn fam]
boy	**un garçon** [œ̃ gaʀsɔ̃]	lady	**une dame** [yn dam]
girl	**une fille** [yn fij]	old people	**les personnes** **âgées** [le pɛʀsɔnzaʒe]
teeneager	**un adolescent** [œ̃ nadɔlesɑ̃]		

Your baby is very sweet.
Votre bébé est très mignon.
[vɔtʀ bebe ɛ tʀɛ miɲɔ̃]

He is..., she looks...
Il est..., elle a l'air...
[il ɛ] [el a lɛʀ]

so..., a bit..., quite...
tellement..., un peu..., assez...
[tɛlmɑ̃] [œ̃ pø] [ase]

fit	**en pleine forme** [ɑ̃ plɛn fɔʀm]	happy	**heureux/-euse** [œʀø] [œʀøz]
tired	**fatigué(e)** [fatige]	handsome, beautiful	**beau/belle** [bo] [bɛl]
kind	**gentil/gentille** [ʒɑ̃ti] [ʒɑ̃tij]	big, tall	**grand(e)** [gʀɑ̃] [gʀɑ̃d]
friendly	**sympathique** [sɛ̃patik]	pretty	**joli(e)** [ʒɔli]
unfriendly	**antipathique** [ɑ̃tipatik]	small	**petit(e)** [pəti] [pətit]
sad	**triste** [tʀist]	funny	**drôle** [dʀol]

Getting Around

In France all roads and railway lines fan out from the central hub of Paris. There are plenty of motorways, but you have to pay tolls on all of them. The country is large by European standards, and many people choose to travel internally by air. More than 140 cities have an airport.

Long-distance trains, especially the express TGV, are fairly reliable, when there isn't a strike *(la grève)*. It is well worth booking your seat; in any case, advance reservation is compulsory for the TGV.

In towns, there are efficient bus or tram services, while in Paris, the best way to get around if you're in a hurry is on the metro (underground train) which whisks you from one station to the next in about a minute. But the city is mostly flat, and ideal for walking. The suburbs are served by the RER, the regional express train.

ASKING YOUR WAY

Be careful when crossing the road: always remember that the traffic drives on the right. French drivers are not renowned for patience or courtesy. But people are likely to be helpful if you lose your way.

I'd like to go to...	**J'aimerais aller à/au...** [ʒɛmərɛzale a/o]
Do you know where... street is?	**Savez-vous où se trouve la rue...?** [save vu u sə tʀuv la ʀy]
Can I walk there?	**Je peux m'y rendre à pied?** [ʒə pø mi ʀɑ̃dʀ a pje]
It's...	**C'est...** [sɛ]

here, over here	**ici, par ici** [isi] [paʀ isi]	opposite	**en face** [ɑ̃ fas]
there, over there	**là, là-bas** [la] [laba]	inside	**à l'intérieur** [a lɛ̃teʀjœʀ]
nearby	**proche** [pʀɔʃ]	outside	**à l'extérieur** [a lɛksteʀjœʀ]
far away	**loin** [lwɛ̃]	between	**entre** [ɑ̃tʀ]
straight ahead	**tout droit** [tu dʀwa]	at the corner of	**au coin de** [o kwɛ̃ də]
on the left	**à gauche** [a goʃ]	close to	**près de** [pʀɛ də]
on the right	**à droite** [a dʀwat]	beside	**à côté de** [a kote də]
upstairs	**en haut** [ɑ̃ o]	before	**avant** [avɑ̃]
downstairs	**en bas** [ɑ̃ ba]	after	**après** [apʀɛ]
beyond	**au-delà** [odəla]	on	**sur** [syʀ]
in front	**devant** [dəvɑ̃]	under	**sous** [su]
behind	**derrière** [dɛʀjɛʀ]	in	**dans** [dɑ̃]

Turn right.	**Tournez à droite.** [turne a drwat]
Cross the street.	**Traversez la rue.** [traverse la ry]
Take the second left.	**Prenez la deuxième à gauche.** [prəne la døzjɛm a goʃ]
Is it far from here?	**Est-ce que c'est loin d'ici?** [ɛskə sɛ lwɛ̃ disi]
It's about...	**C'est à environ...** [sɛt a ɑ̃virɔ̃]
Could you show me the way on the map?	**Pourriez-vous m'indiquer le chemin sur la carte?** [purje vu mɛ̃dike lə ʃəmɛ̃ syr la kart]
Could you draw the way?	**Pourriez-vous me dessiner le chemin à suivre?** [purje vu mə dɛsinə lə ʃəmɛ̃ a sɥivr]
How long does it take to get there?	**Combien de temps faut-il pour s'y rendre?** [kɔ̃bjɛ̃ də tɑ̃ fotil pur si rɑ̃dr]
How can I get there?	**Comment puis-je m'y rendre?** [kɔmɑ̃ pɥiʒ mi rɑ̃dr]

on foot	**à pied** [a pje]	by bus	**en bus** [ɑ̃ bys]
by hitchhiking	**en stop** [ɑ̃ stɔp]	on the underground	**en métro** [ɑ̃ metro]
by bike	**à vélo** [a velo]	by train	**en train** [ɑ̃ trɛ̃]
by car	**en voiture** [ɑ̃ vwatyr]	by plane	**en avion** [ɑ̃navjɔ̃]
by taxi	**en taxi** [ɑ̃ taksi]	by boat	**en bateau** [ɑ̃ bato]

I've lost my way!	**Je me suis perdu(e)!** [ʒə mə sɥi perdy]

IN TOWN

The following list should help you find your way around town or locate a place on the map.

| city centre | **le centre-ville** [lə sɑ̃tʀ vil] | outskirts | **les faubourgs** [le fobuʀ] |
| old town | **la vieille ville** [la vjɛj vil] | suburbs | **la banlieue** [la bɑ̃ljø] |

alley, lane	**la ruelle** [la ʀyɛl]	pedestrian crossing	**le passage pour piétons** [lə pasaʒ puʀ pjetɔ̃]
avenue	**une avenue** [yn avəny]		
crossroads	**le carrefour** [lə kaʀfuʀ]	pedestrian precinct	**la zone piétonne** [la zon pjetɔn]
high street	**la rue principale** [la ʀy pʀɛ̃sipal]	road	**la route** [la ʀut]
path	**le chemin** [lə ʃəmɛ̃]	square	**la place** [la plas]
pavement	**le trottoir** [lə tʀɔtwaʀ]	underpass	**le passage souterrain** [lə pasaʒ sutɛʀɛ̃]

block of flats	**un immeuble** [œ̃nimœbl]	offices	**les bureaux** [le byʀo]
building	**le bâtiment** [lə batimɑ̃]	railway station	**la gare** [la gaʀ]
bus station	**la gare routière** [la gaʀ ʀutjɛʀ]	stadium	**le stade** [lə stad]
church tower	**le clocher** [lə klɔʃe]	town hall	**la Mairie, un Hôtel de Ville** [la mɛʀi] [œ̃notɛl də vil]
house	**la maison** [la mɛzɔ̃]		

abbey	**une abbaye** [yn abɛj]	church	**une église** [yn egliz]
castle	**le château** [lə ʃato]	fountain	**la fontaine** [la fɔ̃tɛn]
cathedral	**la cathédrale** [la katedʀal]	mosque	**la mosquée** [la mɔske]
chapel	**la chapelle** [la ʃapɛl]	museum	**le musée** [lə myze]

36

By taxi

Taxis don't prowl around for business; you have to call one or go to a taxi rank. They also wait outside airports, railway stations, bus terminals and major hotels. There are standard pickup charges, rates per kilometre, and supplements for baggage and a fourth passenger (whom the driver is not obliged to accept).

Where's the nearest taxi rank?	**Où se trouve la station de taxi la plus proche?** [u sə truv la stasjɔ̃ də taksi la ply prɔʃ]
What number should I call for a taxi?	**Quel est le numéro de téléphone des taxis?** [kɛl ɛ lə nymero də telefɔn de taksi]
Hello! I'd like a taxi at...	**Allo! J'aimerais un taxi à/au...** [alo ʒɛmɛre œ̃ taksi a/o]
Could you call a taxi for me?	**Pourriez-vous m'appeler un taxi?** [purje vu mapɔle œ̃ taksi]
I want to go to...	**J'aimerais aller à/au...** [ʒɛmɛrezale a/o]
I've only 10 euros. Is it enough?	**Je n'ai que 10 euros! Est-ce que cela suffit?** [ʒə ne kə dizøro ɛskə səla syfi]
How much does it cost to go to...?	**Combien cela coûte d'aller à/au...?** [kɔ̃bjɛ̃ səla kut dale a/o]
You can put me down here.	**Vous pouvez me déposer ici.** [vu puve mə depoze isi]
Can you wait 5 minutes for me?	**Pourriez-vous m'attendre cinq minutes?** [purje vu matɑ̃dr sɛ̃ minyt]
Could you pick me up at five p.m.?	**Pourriez-vous me prendre à 17 heures?** [purje vu mə prɑ̃dr a diset œr]

BY BUS AND METRO

In Paris, tickets for the underground and the bus are identical; they are mauve and called *ticket t*. They are sold singly or in more economical carnets of 10. Various passes are worth investigating if you are spending several days in the capital.

Where's the nearest underground station?	**Où se trouve la station de métro la plus proche?** [u sə tʀuv la stasjɔ̃ də metʀo la ply pʀɔʃ]
Where's the bus stop?	**Où se trouve l'arrêt de bus?** [u sə tʀuv laʀɛ də bys]
Which line should I take for...?	**Quelle ligne dois-je prendre pour...?** [kɛl liɲ dwaʒ pʀɑ̃dʀ puʀ]
Do I have to change lines?	**Est-ce que je dois changer de ligne?** [ɛskə ʒə dwa ʃɑ̃ʒe də liɲ]
Where can I buy a ticket?	**Où puis-je acheter un billet?** [u pɥiʒ aʃte œ̃ bije]
I'd like a carnet.	**J'aimerais un carnet de billets.** [jɛmə ʀɛzœ̃ kaʀne də bije]
When does the next bus leave?	**Quand part le prochain bus?** [kɑ̃ paʀ lə pʀɔʃɛ̃ bys]
What time is the last one?	**A quelle heure est le dernier?** [a kel œʀ ɛ lə dɛʀnje]
Is this the right bus/train to...?	**Est-ce bien le bon bus/la rame pour...?** [ɛsə bjɛ̃ lə bɔ̃ bys/la ʀam puʀ]
How many stops are there to...?	**Combien d'arrêts y a-t-il jusqu'à...?** [kɔ̃bjɛ̃ daʀe jatil ʒuska]
Could you tell me when to get off?	**Pourriez-vous me dire quand je dois descendre?** [puʀje vu mə diʀ kɑ̃ ʒə dwa dɛsɑ̃dʀ]

By Train

If you buy your rail tickets in France, remember to punch them in the orange machine at the platform entrance just before you get on the train.

Where's the station?	**Où se trouve la gare?** [u sə tʀuv la gaʀ]
Where's the ticket office?	**Où se trouve le guichet?** [u sə tʀuv lə giʃe]
What time's the next train to...?	**A quelle heure est le prochain train pour...?** [a kel œʀ ɛ lə pʀɔʃɛ̃ tʀɛ̃ puʀ]
How much is a ticket to...?	**Combien coûte un billet pour...?** [kɔ̃bjɛ̃ kut œ̃ bije puʀ]
I'd like to book a seat.	**J'aimerais réserver une place.** [ʒɛməʀɛ ʀezeʀve yn plas]
single/return	**aller simple/aller-retour** [ale sɛ̃pl] [ale ʀətuʀ]
1st class/2nd class	**première classe/deuxième classe** [pʀəmjeʀ klas] [døzjɛm klas]
intercity/local train	**le train express/un omnibus** [lə tʀɛ̃ ɛkspʀes] [œ̃nɔmnibys]
sleeper	**le wagon-lit** [lə vagɔ̃li]
What platform does my train leave from?	**De quel quai part mon train?** [də kel ke paʀ mɔ̃ tʀɛ̃]
Where's the left luggage office?	**Où se trouve la consigne?** [u sə tʀuv la kɔ̃siɲ]
Is this seat free?	**Cette place est-elle libre?** [set plas ɛtɛl libʀ]
I've lost my ticket!	**J'ai perdu mon billet!** [ʒe peʀdy mɔ̃ bije]
I've missed my train!	**J'ai raté le train!** [ʒe ʀate lə tʀɛ̃]

BY PLANE

You can buy plane tickets in a travel agency, the airline office or even at the airport, if you want to risk a standby. You could also find an Internet café and buy your tickets online.

I'd like to buy a plane ticket...	**J'aimerais acheter un billet d'avion...** [ʒɛmərɛzaʃte œ̃ bije davjɔ̃]
... economy/business class	**... en classe économique/ affaires** [ã klas ekɔnɔmik/afɛʀ]
... first class	**... en première classe** [ã pʀəmjɛʀ klas]
window/aisle	**la fenêtre/le couloir** [la fənɛtʀ] [lə kulwaʀ]
How can I get to the airport?	**Comment puis-je me rendre à l'aéroport?** [kɔmã pɥiz mə ʀãdʀa laeʀɔpɔʀ]
arrivals/departures	**arrivées/départs** [aʀive] [depaʀ]
Where's the check-in desk?	**Où se trouve l'enregistrement?** [u sə tʀuv lãʀəʒistʀəmã]
boarding pass	**la carte d'embarquement** [la kaʀt dãbaʀkəmã]
Where are the duty-free shops?	**Où se trouvent les magasins hors taxes?** [u sə tʀuv le magazɛ̃ ɔʀ taks]
Have you anything for air sickness?	**Avez-vous un médicament contre le mal de l'air?** [ave vu œ̃ medikamã kɔ̃tʀ lə mal də lɛʀ]
take-off/landing	**le décollage/l'atterrissage** [le dekɔlaʒ] [lateʀisaʒ]
My bags aren't there.	**Mes bagages ne sont pas arrivés.** [me bagaʒ nə sɔ̃ pazaʀive]

BY BOAT

France doesn't stop at the coast. From Marseille, you can take a ferry to rugged Corsica, and there are lots of smaller islands to explore around Brittany, in the Atlantic and Mediterranean.

Where's the ferry embarkation point?	**Où se trouve le départ des ferries?** [u sə tʀuv lə depaʀ de fɛʀi]
Where can I buy a ticket for the ferry?	**Où puis-je acheter un billet pour le ferry?** [u pɥiʒ aʃte œ̃ bije puʀ lə fɛʀi]
Have you a connection with...?	**Avez-vous une liaison sur...** [ave vu yn ljɛzɔ̃ syʀ]
What time does it arrive?	**A quelle heure arrive-t-il à destination?** [a kɛl œʀ aʀivətil a dɛstinasjɔ̃]
I'd like to book a cabin.	**J'aimerais réserver une cabine.** [ʒɛməʀɛ ʀezɛʀve yn kabin]
single/double	**simple/double** [sɛ̃pl] [duhl]
I'm travelling with a...	**Je voyage avec...** [ʒə vvajaʒ avɛk]
... caravan	**... une caravane** [yn kaʀavan]
... campervan	**... un mobile home** [œ̃ mɔbilom]
... car	**... une voiture** [yn vvatyʀ]
life boat/lifejacket/lifebelt	**le canot/le gilet de sauvetage/ la bouée de sauvetage** [lə kano] [lə ʒile də sovətaʒ] [la bue də sovətaʒ]
on deck	**sur le pont** [syʀ lə pɔ̃]
Man overboard!	**Un homme à la mer!** [œnɔm a la mɛʀ]

CAR HIRE

If you want to hire a car in France, don't forget that you'll need an international driving licence (*permis de conduire international*), and your credit card.

I'd like to hire a...	**J'aimerais louer...** [ʒɛməʀɛ lue]
... bicycle/motorbike/car/van	**... un vélo/une moto/une voiture/une camionnette** [œ̃ velo] [yn mɔto] [yn vwatyʀ] [yn kamjɔnɛt]
mini/mid-size/large	**petit/moyen/grand** [pəti] [mwajɛ̃] [gʀɑ̃]
manual/automatic	**manuel/automatique** [manɥɛl] [ɔtɔmatik]
with air-conditioning	**avec climatisation** [avɛk klimatizasjɔ̃]
What models can you offer?	**Quels modèles proposez-vous?** [kel mɔdɛl pʀɔpoze vu]
How much is it per day/week?	**C'est combien par jour/semaine?** [sɛ kɔ̃bjɛ̃ paʀ juʀ/səmɛn]
Do I have to leave a deposit?	**Dois-je laisser une caution?** [dwaʒ lɛse yn kosjɔ̃]
Is insurance included?	**L'assurance est-elle incluse?** [lasyʀɑ̃s ɛtɛl ɛ̃klyz]
What does this insurance cover?	**Que couvre cette assurance?** [kə kuvʀ sɛt asyʀɑ̃s]
legal liability, third party, public liability	**la responsabilité civile** [la ʀɛspɔ̃sabilite sivil]
theft protection	**l'assurance contre le vol** [lasyʀɑ̃s kɔ̃tʀ lə vol]
collision damage waiver	**la réduction de responsabilité en cas de dommages** [la ʀedyksjɔ̃ də ʀɛspɔ̃sabilite ɑ̃ ka də dɔmaʒ]

personal accidence insurance	**assurance accidents** [asyʀɑ̃s aksidɑ̃]
compulsory/optional	**obligatoire/facultatif** [ɔbligatwaʀ] [fakyltatif]
excess charge	**la franchise** [la fʀɑ̃ʃiz]
unlimited mileage	**le kilométrage illimité** [lə kilɔmetʀaʒ ilimite]
additional driver	**un conducteur supplémentaire** [œ̃ kɔ̃dyktœʀ syplemɑ̃tɛʀ]
Have you a form in English?	**Avez-vous un formulaire en anglais?** [ave vu œ̃ fɔʀmylɛʀ ɑ̃nɑ̃glɛ]
What kind of petrol does it take?	**Que faut-il mettre comme carburant?** [kə fotil mɛtʀ kɔm kaʀbyʀɑ̃]
unleaded/4-star/diesel	**sans plomb/super/gazole** [sɑ̃ plɔ̃] [sypɛʀ] [gazɔl]
Do I have to return the car with a full tank?	**Dois-je rendre la voiture avec un plein d'essence?** [dwaʒ ʀɑ̃dʀ la vwatyʀ avɛk œ̃ plɛ̃ dɛsɑ̃s]
I need a child seat.	**J'ai besoin d'un siège pour enfant.** [ʒe bəzwɛ̃ dœ̃ sjɛʒ puʀɑ̃fɑ̃]
Could you give me a...	**Pouvez-vous me donner...?** [puve vu mə dɔne]
... road map	**... une carte routière** [yn kaʀt ʀutjɛʀ]
... highway code	**... un code de la route** [œ̃ kɔd də la ʀut]
Can I return the car in another town?	**Puis-je rendre le véhicule à un autre endroit?** [pɥiʒ ʀɑ̃dʀ lə veikyl a œn otʀ ɑ̃dʀwa]

ON THE ROAD

The roads are well signposted and easy to follow. Motorways are indicated by blue panels and are designated by the letter A; they also have names, La Languedocienne, l'Autoroute du Soleil, etc. They are privately owned and tolls are charged: you pick up a ticket as you enter the *station de péage*, and hand it in at the window when you leave. The price depends on the distance covered and the size of your vehicle, and you can pay in cash or with your credit card. The lanes marked with a big letter "t" are for pass-holders only.

Am I on the right road for...?	**Suis-je sur la bonne route pour...?** [sɥiʒ syʀ la bɔn ʀut puʀ]	
Follow this road for 10 kilometres.	**Suivez cette route sur 10 kilomètres.** [sɥive sɛt ʀut syʀ di kilomɛtʀ]	
Go back to...	**Retournez en arrière jusqu'à/au...** [ʀətuʀne ɑ̃naʀjɛʀ ʒyska/o]	
Drive north	**Roulez en direction du nord** [ʀule ɑ̃ diʀɛksjɔ̃ dy nɔʀ]	
... south/east/west	**... du sud/de l'est/de l'ouest** [dy syd] [də lɛst] [də lwɛst]	

bend, turning	**le virage** [lə viʀaʒ]	fork, junction	**la bifurcation** [la bifyʀkasjɔ̃]
bridge	**le pont** [lə pɔ̃]	main road	**route principale** [ʀut pʀɛsipal]
bypass	**la route de contournement** [la ʀut də kɔ̃tuʀnəmɑ̃]	ring-road	**le périphérique** [lə peʀiferik]
diversion	**la déviation** [la devjasjɔ̃]	roundabout	**le rond-point** [lə ʀɔ̃pwɛ̃]
dual carriageway	**la route à deux voies** [la ʀut a dø vwa]	secondary road	**la route secondaire** [la ʀut segɔ̃dɛʀ]
		tunnel	**le tunnel** [lə tynɛl]

Where's the petrol station?	**Où se trouve la station-service?** [u sə tʀuv la stasjɔ̃sɛʀvis]
Full tank, please.	**Le plein, s'il vous plaît.** [lə plɛ̃ silvuplɛ]
I'm at pump number...	**Je suis à la colonne numéro...** [ʒə sɥiza la kɔlɔn nymeʀo]
Could you check the...?	**Pourriez-vous vérifier...?** [puʀjevu veʀifje]
... battery	**... la batterie** [la batʀi]
... brake fluid	**... le liquide de freins** [lə likid də fʀɛ̃]
... oil level	**... le niveau d'huile** [lə nivo dɥil]
... tyre pressure	**... la pression des pneus** [la pʀɛsjɔ̃ de pnø]
My car's broken down.	**Ma voiture est en panne.** [ma vwatyʀ ɛtɑ̃ pan]
I've run out of petrol.	**Je suis en panne d'essence.** [ʒə sɥizɑ̃ pan dɛsɑ̃s]
I've a flat tyre.	**J'ai crevé un pneu.** [ʒe kʀəve œ̃ pnø]
The battery's flat.	**La batterie est à plat.** [la batʀi ɛta pla]
There's a problem with the...	**Il y a un problème avec...** [ilja œ̃ pʀɔblɛm avɛk]

shock absorbers	**les amortisseurs** [lezamɔʀtisœ]	brakes	**les freins** [le fʀɛ̃]
gear box	**la boîte de vitesses** [la bwat də vitɛs]	engine	**le moteur** [lə motœʀ]
		exhaust pipe	**le pot d'échappement** [lə po deʃapəmɑ̃]
steering	**la direction** [la diʀɛksjɔ̃]		

I'm looking for a car park.	**Je cherche un parking.** [ʒə ʃɛrʃ œ̃ parkiŋ]
I'm looking for a garage.	**Je cherche un garage.** [ʒə ʃɛrʃ œ̃ garaʒ]
Please call a breakdown truck.	**Appelez une dépanneuse, s'il vous plaît.** [apəle yn depanøz silvuplɛ]
Can it be repaired quickly?	**Est-il possible de faire les réparations rapidement?** [ɛtil pɔsibl də fɛr le reparasjɔ̃ rapidmɑ̃]
When will the repairs be done?	**Quand est-ce que les réparations seront terminées?** [kɑ̃tɛskə le reparasjɔ̃ sərɔ̃ tɛrmine]
Could you call the rental firm?	**Pouvez-vous contacter l'agence de location?** [puve vu kɔ̃takte laʒɑ̃s də lɔkasjɔ̃]
I need another car.	**J'ai besoin d'une autre voiture.** [ʒe bəzwɛ̃ dyn otrə vwatyr]
I've had an accident.	**J'ai eu un accident.** [ʒe y œ̃naksidɑ̃]
jointly agreed statement	**un constat à l'amiable** [œ̃ kɔ̃sta a lamjabl]

ITINÉRAIRES BIS

During peak periods, especially the dreaded weekend at the end of
July and beginning of August when the whole country is going on
holiday or driving back home, the motorways are best avoided. You
will notice big green signs indicating *Itinéraires bis*; these are alter-
native routes which will often take you through scenic countryside.

Accommodation

In France, hotels are officially graded from zero stars to four-star luxury (****L). At the top of the spectrum are the *Relais et Châteaux*, about 150 prestigious country estates and converted castles. All are of a very high standard and offer top cuisine.

Along the same lines are the *Relais du Silence*, where you can count on a tranquil setting. *Logis de France*, another chain, offers comfortable family-run hotels throughout the country. If you fancy self-catering, consider a *gîte*; these are cottages or flats in the owner's house, or part of a farm, and extremely popular.

In hotels, breakfast is usually charged extra; an *hôtel garni* does not have a dining room.

In July and August it's essential to book in advance. You may have to pay a deposit (*les arrhes*) on booking.

FINDING A ROOM

To find a room once you're on the spot, go to the local tourist information office, the *Maison de la France* or the *Syndicat d'Initiative*, as they have lists of all the accommodation available. A good way of meeting French people is to stay in a *chambre d'hôte*, literally guest room, similar to Bed and Breakfast (also called *Café couette*).

Can you recommend a hotel?	**Pouvez-vous me conseiller un hôtel?** [puve vu mə kɔ̃sɛje œ̃notɛl]
I'm looking for a guesthouse.	**Je cherche une pension.** [ʒə ʃɛrʃ yn pɑ̃sjɔ̃]
bed and breakfast	**une chambre d'hôte** [yn ʃɑ̃bʀ dot]
youth hostel	**une auberge de jeunesse** [yn obɛʀʒ də ʒønɛs]
not too expensive	**pas trop chère** [pa tʀo ʃɛʀ]
Is it quiet?	**Est-ce que c'est un endroit calme?** [ɛskə sɛtœ̃nɑ̃dʀwa kalm]
Do you have any rooms free?	**Avez-vous une chambre de libre?** [ave vu yn ʃɑ̃bʀ də libʀ]
How much is it per night?	**Combien coûte-t-elle par nuit?** [kɔ̃bjɛ̃ kutətɛl paʀ nɥi]
Is breakfast included?	**Le petit-déjeuner est-il compris?** [lə pəti deʒøne ɛtil kɔ̃pʀi]
half board/full board	**demi-pension/pension complète** [dəmi pɑ̃sjɔ̃] [pɑ̃sjɔ̃ kɔ̃plɛt]
Can I see the room?	**Puis-je voir la chambre?** [pɥiʒ vwaʀ la ʃɑ̃bʀ]
That's fine, I'll take it.	**D'accord, je la prends.** [dakɔʀ ʒə la pʀɑ̃]

CHECKING IN

When you arrive at your hotel, you will have to fill in a registration form, and you may have to hand over your credit card for an imprint to be taken.

Do you know where the Palace Hotel is?	**Savez-vous où se trouve l'Hôtel Palace?** [save vu u sə truv lotɛl palas]
I've booked a room.	**J'ai réservé une chambre.** [ʒe rezɛrve yn ʃɑ̃br]
I'm staying for three nights.	**Je reste trois nuits.** [ʒə rɛst trwa nɥi]
I'd like a single/double room with...	**J'aimerais une chambre simple/double avec...** [ʒɛmərɛ yn ʃɑ̃br sɛ̃pl/dubl avɛk]
... a double bed/twin beds	**... un grand lit/deux lits** [œ̃ grɑ̃ li] [dø li]
... a shower/bath	**... douche/bain** [duʃ] [bɛ̃]
... a sea view	**... vue sur la mer** [vy syr la mɛr]
Could I change rooms?	**Est-ce que je pourrais changer de chambre?** [ɛskə ʒə purɛ ʃɑ̃ʒe də ʃɑ̃br]
Could you...	**Pouvez-vous...** [puve vu]
... take my bags up to the room?	**... monter mes bagages dans la chambre?** [mɔ̃te me bagaʒ dɑ̃ la ʃɑ̃br]
... add an extra bed?	**...ajouter un lit supplémentaire?** [aʒute œ̃ li syplemɑ̃tɛr]
... unlock the minibar?	**... déverrouiller le minibar?** [devɛruje lə minibar]
... connect the phone?	**... brancher le téléphone?** [brɑ̃ʃe lə telefɔn]

AT THE HOTEL

Ask at the hotel reception if you need anything—a taxi, theatre tickets, recommendation for a good restaurant, a baby-sitter, and so on.

What time is the front door closed?	**A quelle heure fermez-vous la porte d'entrée?** [a kɛlœr fɛrme vu la pɔrt dɑ̃tre]
What time is breakfast served?	**A quelle heure servez-vous le petit-déjeuner?** [a kɛlœr sɛrve vu lə pəti deʒøne]
Where's the dining room?	**Où est la salle à manger?** [u ɛ la sal a mɑ̃ʒe]
I'd like the key to room no. 7.	**J'aimerais la clé de la chambre numéro sept.** [ʒɛmərɛ la kle də la ʃɑ̃br nymero sɛt]
I've lost the key.	**J'ai perdu la clé.** [ʒe pɛrdy la kle]
I'm locked out of my room.	**Je suis enfermé dehors.** [ʒə sɥi ɑ̃fɛrme dəɔr]
My room hasn't been made up.	**Ma chambre n'a pas été faite.** [ma ʃɑ̃br na pazete fɛt]
Can I leave my papers in the safe?	**Est-ce que je peux déposer mes papiers dans le coffre-fort?** [ɛskə ʒə pø depoze me papje dɑ̃ lə kɔfrəfɔr]
Could you give me a wake-up call at 8 a.m.?	**Pouvez-vous me réveiller à 8 heures demain matin?** [puve vu mə reveje a ɥit œr dəmɛ̃ matɛ̃]
I'd like to stay an extra night.	**J'aimerais rester une nuit de plus.** [ʒɛmərɛ rɛste yn nɥi də ply]
What time do I need to check out?	**A quelle heure dois-je libérer la chambre?** [a kɛl œr dwaʒ libere la ʃɑ̃br]

Could you prepare my bill?	**Pourriez-vous préparer ma note?** [puʀje vu pʀepaʀe ma nɔt]
I didn't take anything from the minibar.	**Je n'ai rien pris dans le minibar.** [ʒə ne ʀjɛ̃ pʀi dɑ̃ lə minibaʀ]
Can I leave my luggage here till 3 o'clock?	**Est-ce que je peux laisser mes bagages ici jusqu'à 15 heures?** [ɛskə ʒə pø lɛse me bagaʒ isi ʒyska kɛz œʀ]

Maybe something's wrong with your room, or you've left an indispensable article behind? Call Reception.

The window's stuck.	**La fenêtre est coincée.** [la fənɛtʀ ɛ kwɛ̃se]
The tap's dripping.	**Le robinet fuit.** [lə ʀɔbine fɥi]
The toilet won't flush.	**La chasse d'eau ne fonctionne pas.** [la ʃas do nə fɔ̃ksjɔn pa]
The light doesn't work.	**La lumière ne fonctionne pas.** [la lymjɛʀ nə fɔ̃ksjɔn pa]
How do you switch the air conditioning on/off?	**Comment est-ce qu'on allume/éteint la climatisation?** [kɔmɑ̃ ɛskɔ̃ alym/etɛ̃ la klimatizasjɔ̃]
The radiator's making a funny noise.	**Le radiateur fait un bruit bizarre.** [lə ʀadjatœʀ fɛt œ̃ bʀɥi bizaʀ]
The lift is stuck between the 3rd and 4th floors.	**L'ascenseur est coincé entre le 3ème et le 4ème étage.** [lasɑ̃sœʀ ɛ kwɛ̃se ɑ̃tʀə lə tʀwazjɛm e lə katʀjɛm etaʒ]
Can I drink the tap water?	**L'eau du robinet est-elle potable?** [lo dy ʀɔbine ɛtɛl pɔtabl]

adaptor	**un adaptateur** [œ̃ nadaptatœʀ]	ironing board	**une planche à repasser** [yn plɑ̃ʃ a ʀəpase]
ash tray	**un cendrier** [œ̃ sɑ̃dʀie]	laundry	**une blanchisserie** [yn blɑ̃ʃisʀi]
bath plug	**une bonde** [yn bɔ̃d]		
blanket	**une couverture** [yn kuvɛʀtyʀ]	light bulb	**une ampoule** [yn ɑ̃pul]
chair	**une chaise** [yn ʃɛz]	pillow	**un oreiller** [œ̃ nɔʀɛje]
clothes hanger	**un cintre** [œ̃ sɛ̃tʀ]	plug	**une prise mâle** [yn pʀiz mal]
curtains	**les rideaux** [le ʀido]	razor socket	**une prise pour rasoir électrique** [yn pʀiz puʀ ʀazwaʀ elɛktʀik]
dry-cleaning	**le nettoyage à sec** [lə nɛtwajaʒ a sɛk]	sheet	**un drap** [œ̃ dʀa]
duvet	**une couette** [yn kwɛt]	socket	**une prise femelle** [yn pʀiz famɛl]
eiderdown	**un édredon** [œ̃ nedʀədɔ̃]		
hair drier	**un sèche-cheveux** [œ̃ sɛʃ ʃəvø]	toilet paper	**le papier toilette** [lə papje twalɛt]
hot-water bottle	**une bouillote** [yn bujɔt]	towel	**un drap de bain** [œ̃ dʀa də bɛ̃]
iron	**un fer à repasser** [œ̃ fɛʀ a ʀəpase]	wash basin	**le lavabo** [lə lavabo]

CONTINENTAL BREAKFAST

In small hotels, breakfast usually consists of a choice of coffee, tea or hot chocolate, a glass of fruit juice, croissants or other pastry, a length of crusty baguette, butter, jam and honey. Large hotels often present a full-scale buffet with various cereals and milk, ham, cheese, fruit and yoghurt, enough to set you up for a hard day's sightseeing.

CAMPING

Don't put your tent up just anywhere. *Le camping sauvage*, as it is called in French, is strictly forbidden. Campsites are rated in categories from one to four stars; for a list, see www.campingfrance.com

Is there a campsite in the region?	**Y a-t-il un terrain de camping dans la région?** [jatil ɶ̃ tɛʀɛ̃ də kɑ̃piŋ dɑ̃ la ʀeʒjɔ̃]
Is camping allowed here?	**Est-il permis de camper ici?** [ɛtil pɛʀmi də kɑ̃pe isi]
Can we light a fire here?	**Est-ce qu'on peut faire un feu ici?** [ɛskɔ̃ pø fɛʀ ɶ̃ fø isi]
Do you have any free spaces?	**Vous reste-t-il des emplacements de libre?** [vu ʀɛstətil dezɑ̃plasmɑ̃ də libʀ]
I'd like a pitch for a...	**J'aimerais un emplacement pour...** [ʒɛməʀezɶ̃ ɑ̃plasmɑ̃ puʀ]
... tent/car	**... une tente/une voiture** [yn tɑ̃t] [yn vwatyʀ]
... caravan/campervan	**... une caravane/un mobile home** [yn kaʀavan] [ɶ̃ mɔbilom]
How much is it per day/week?	**Combien ça coûte par jour/semaine?** [kɔ̃bjɛ̃ sa kut paʀ juʀ/səmɛn]
Where are the washing facilities?	**Où se trouvent les sanitaires?** [u sə tʀuv le sanitɛʀ]
Where's the power point/water stand?	**Où est-ce que l'on branche l'électricité/l'eau?** [u ɛskə lɔ̃ bʀɑ̃ʃ lelɛktʀisite/lo]
Where can I get butane gas?	**Où puis-je trouver du gaz butane?** [u pɥiʒ tʀuve dy gɑz bytan]

53

Where can I dry my things?	**Où puis-je faire sécher mes affaires?** [u pɥiʒ fɛʀ seʃe mezafɛʀ]
Is there a... nearby?	**Y a-t-il... dans le coin?** [jatil] [dɑ̃ lə kwɛ̃]
... grocery	**... une épicerie** [yn episʀi]
... swimming pool	**... une piscine** [yn pisin]
... playground	**... une place de jeux** [yn plas də ʒø]
I'd like another pitch.	**J'aimerais changer d'emplacement.** [ʒɛməʀɛ ʃɑ̃ʒe dɑ̃plasmɑ̃]
This one's too close to the dustbins.	**Celui-ci est trop près des poubelles.** [səlɥi si ɛ tʀo pʀe de pubɛl]
The ground is uneven.	**Le terrain n'est pas plat.** [lə tɛʀɛ̃ nɛ pa pla]
My tent's leaking!	**Ma tente prend l'eau!** [ma tɑ̃t pʀɑ̃ lo]
Have you anything to repair it?	**Avez-vous de quoi la réparer?** [ave vu də kwa la ʀepaʀe]

battery	**pile** [pil]		rope	**corde** [kɔʀd]
camping stove	**réchaud à gaz** [ʀeʃo a gɑz]		saucepan	**casserole** [kasəʀɔl]
firelighters	**allume-feu** [alym fø]		sleeping bag	**sac de couchage** [sak də kuʃaʒ]
frying pan	**poêle** [pwal]		stake	**sardine, piquet** [saʀdin] [pike]
ground sheet	**tapis de sol** [tapi də sɔl]		toggle	**tendeur** [tɑ̃dœʀ]
matches	**allumettes** [alymɛt]		torch	**lampe de poche** [lɑ̃p də pɔʃ]

Dining Out

The French take food and cooking extremely seriously, and whatever your budget you will have wonderful experiences dining out.

One of the joys of travelling is discovering regional specialities; ask about local fare and look out for *tables d'hôte*, where excellent, inexpensive meals are provided in people's homes.

Lunch, taken at any time from noon to about 1.30 p.m., is a serious affair, generally a cooked meal. Dinner can run to four courses or more. In restaurants, most people sit down to eat at about 8 or 9 p.m., though in private homes and country restaurants, they may dine earlier, at 7 or 7.30 p.m.

Apart from French food, you will see many "ethnic" restaurants; among the best are Vietnamese, Cambodian, Lebanese, North African and East European. Japanese cuisine is increasingly popular.

CHOOSING A RESTAURANT

If you intend to dine out in a classy restaurant, make sure you book in advance. Some places are so renowned you need to reserve a table several weeks ahead.

I'm hungry!	**J'ai faim!** [ʒe fɛ̃]
Could you recommend a good restaurant?	**Pouvez-vous me conseiller un bon restaurant?** [puve vu mə kɔ̃sɛje œ̃ bɔ̃ ʀɛstoʀɑ̃]
vegetarian/halal/kosher	**végétarien/halal/casher** [veʒetaʀjɛ̃] [halal] [kaʃɛʀ]
Do you know a bistrot with good food?	**Connaissez-vous un bistrot où l'on mange bien?** [kɔnɛse vu œ̃ bistro u lɔ̃ mɑ̃ʒ bjɛ̃]
I'd like to try some local specialities.	**J'aimerais goûter des spécialités locales.** [ʒɛməʀɛ gute de spesjalite lɔkal]
We could try... food.	**On pourrait essayer la cuisine...** [ɔ̃ puʀɛ ɛsɛje la kɥizin]

Belgian	**belge** [bɛlʒ]	Moroccan	**marocaine** [maʀɔkɛn]
Cambodian	**cambodgienne** [kɑ̃bɔdʒjɛn]	Portuguese	**portugaise** [pɔʀtygɛz]
Chinese	**chinoise** [ʃinwaz]	Russian	**russe** [ʀys]
Greek	**grecque** [gʀɛk]	Spanish	**espagnole** [ɛspaɲɔl]
Italian	**italienne** [italjɛn]	Thai	**thaïe** [tai]
Japanese	**japonaise** [ʒapɔnɛz]	Turkish	**turque** [tyʀk]
Lebanese	**libanaise** [libanɛz]	Vietnamese	**vietnamienne** [vjɛtnamjɛn]

56

We could settle for a takeaway.	**On pourrait prendre quelque chose à emporter.**	
	[ɔ̃ puʀɛ pʀɑ̃dʀ kɛlkə ʃoz a ɑ̃pɔʀte]	
How about a sandwich?	**Et si on prenait un sandwich?**	
	[e si ɔ̃ pʀənɛ œ̃ sɑ̃dwitʃ]	
We could have a picnic.	**On pourrait faire un pique-nique.**	
	[ɔ̃ puʀɛ fɛʀ œ̃ piknik]	
Let's find a...	**Cherchons...**	
	[ʃɛʀʃɔ̃]	

bakery	**une boulangerie** [yn bulɑ̃ʒʀi]	health food shop	**un magasin diététique** [œ̃ magazɛ̃ djetɛtik]
butchers	**une boucherie** [yn buʃʀi]	market	**un marché** [œ̃ maʀʃe]
cake shop	**une pâtisserie** [yn pɑtisʀi]		
cheese shop	**une fromagerie** [yn fʀomaʒʀi]	snack bar	**un snack** [œ̃ snak]
delicatessen	**un traiteur** [œ̃ tʀɛtœʀ]	supermarket	**un supermarché** [œ̃ sypɛʀmaʀʃe]
fishmongers	**une poissonnerie** [yn pwasɔnʀi]	sweet shop	**une confiserie** [yn kɔ̃fizʀi]
grocery	**une épicerie** [yn episʀi]	wine bar	**un bar à vin** [œ̃ baʀ a vɛ̃]

COFFEE IN A CAFÉ

If you just ask the waiter for *un café*, you will be served a tiny cup of thick, black liquid. For something more satisfying, ask for *un grand café*, and you will get twice as much. If you want it milky, ask for *un crème*. Tea will be of the teabag kind, served in a glass mug, unless you go to an elegant *salon de thé* where you can choose from all kinds of delicious flavours, presented in a pot *(une théière)*.

AT THE RESTAURANT

By law, all restaurants must display menus outside, showing the prices. There is generally a range of good-value set menus, or you can choose your courses *à la carte*.

Can we still have lunch/dinner?	**Peut-on encore manger à cette heure-ci?** [pøtɔ̃ ɑ̃kɔʀ mɑ̃ʒe a sɛt œʀ si]
Have you a free table?	**Avez-vous une table de libre?** [ave vu yn tabl də libʀ]
We'd like a table in the non-smoking area.	**On aimerait une table dans le coin non-fumeurs.** [ɔ̃nɛməʀɛ yn tabl dɑ̃ lə kwɛ̃ nɔ̃fymœʀ]
I've booked a table for Mr Michel.	**J'ai réservé une table au nom de M. Michel.** [ʒe ʀezɛʀve yn tabl o nɔ̃ də məsjø miʃɛl]
menu/wine list	**le menu/la carte des vins** [lə məny] [la kaʀt de vɛ̃]
The bill, please.	**L'addition, s'il vous plaît.** [ladisjɔ̃ silvuplɛ]
We'd like more bread/butter.	**On aimerait encore du pain/du beurre.** [ɔ̃nɛməʀɛ ɑ̃kɔʀ dy pɛ̃/dy bœʀ]
Could you bring me a/an...	**Pourriez-vous m'apporter...** [puʀje vu mapɔʀte]

cup	**une tasse** [yn tas]	plate	**une assiette** [yn asjɛt]
fork	**une fourchette** [yn fuʀʃɛt]	saucer	**une soucoupe** [yn sukup]
glass	**un verre** [œ̃ vɛʀ]	serviette	**une serviette** [yn sɛʀvjɛt]
knife	**un couteau** [œ̃ kuto]	spoon	**une cuiller** [yn kɥijɛʀ]

At lunchtime, the *menu du jour* generally consists of three courses: *entrée*, *plat du jour* and *dessert*. A carafe of house wine is sometimes included (*vin compris*).

What's the day's special?	**Quel est le plat du jour?** [kɛl ɛ lə pla dy juʀ]
What do you recommend?	**Que nous recommandez-vous?** [kə nu ʀəkɔmɑ̃de vu]
appetizers	**hors-d'œuvre** [ɔʀ dœvʀ]
starters	**entrées** [ɑ̃tʀe]
main dish	**plat principal** [pla pʀɛ̃sipal]
side dish	**garniture** [gaʀnityʀ]
dessert	**dessert** [desɛʀ]
drinks	**boissons** [bwasɔ̃]
a small portion	**une petite portion** [yn pətit pɔʀsjɔ̃]

Condiments

black pepper	**poivre noir** [pwavʀ nwaʀ]	(olive) oil	**huile (d'olive)** [ɥil dɔliv]
ketchup	**sauce tomate, ketchup** [sos tɔmat] [kɛtʃəp]	salt	**sel** [sɛl]
		sugar	**sucre** [sykʀ]
mayonnaise	**mayonnaise** [majɔnɛz]	vinegar	**vinaigre** [vinɛgʀ]
mustard	**moutarde** [mutaʀd]	white pepper	**poivre blanc** [pwavʀ blɑ̃]

A LA CARTE

In this section, we have listed the French words in the first column, to help you decipher the menu.

Starters

anchois [ɑ̃ʃwa]	anchovy	**jambon** [ʒɑ̃bɔ̃]	ham
andouille, andouillette [ɑ̃duj] [ɑ̃dujɛt]	chitterling sausage	**langouste** [lɑ̃gust]	spiny lobster
asperge [aspɛrʒ]	asparagus	**moules** [mul]	mussels
bouillon [bujɔ̃]	broth	**œuf dur** [œf dyr]	hard-boiled egg
calmar [kalmar]	squid	**olives** [ɔliv]	olives
cœur d'artichaut [kœr dartiʃo]	artichoke heart	**oursin** [ursɛ̃]	sea-urchin
coquille Saint-Jacques [kɔkij sɛ̃ ʒak]	scallop	**palourde** [palurd]	clams
crabe [krab]	crab	**pommes de terre en salade** [pɔm de tɛr ɑ̃ salad]	potato salad
crevette [krəvɛt]	shrimp	**potage** [pɔtaʒ]	soup
cuisses de grenouille [kɥis də grənuj]	frogs' legs	**poulpe** [pulp]	octopus
écrevisse [ekrəvis]	crayfish	**quenelles** [kənɛl]	meat or fish dumplings
encornet [ɑ̃kɔrne]	squid	**rillettes** [rijɛt]	potted pork, duck or goose
escargot [ɛskargo]	snail	**salade de tomates** [salad də tɔmat]	tomato salad
foie gras [fwa gra]	goose or duck liver	**saucisson** [sosisɔ̃]	dried sausage
fruits de mer [frɥi də mɛr]	seafood	**saumon fumé** [somɔ̃ fyme]	smoked salmon
homard [ɔmar]	lobster	**seiche** [sɛʃ]	cuttlefish
huîtres [ɥitr]	oysters	**sot-l'y-laisse** [soliɛs]	chicken oysters
		soupe [sup]	soup

60

Meat and poultry

If you order a steak, the waiter will ask you if you want it *bleu* (very rare), *saignant* (rare) or *à point* (medium). If you want it well done, say *bien cuit*.

agneau [aɲo]	lamb	**côtelette** [kotlɛt]	chop
alouette [aluɛt]	skylark	**dinde** [dɛ̃d]	turkey
bécasse [bekas]	woodcock	**entrecôte** [ɑ̃trəkot]	beef steak cut from between the ribs
biftek [biftɛk]	steak	**escalope** [ɛskalɔp]	scallop (thin slice), generally veal
bœuf [bœf]	Beef		
boudin blanc [budɛ̃ blɑ̃]	white pudding	**faisan** [fəzɑ̃]	pheasant
boudin noir [budɛ̃ nwar]	black pudding (blood sausage)	**filet mignon** [filə miɲɔ̃]	pork/veal fillet
caille [kaj]	quail	**foie** [fwa]	liver
canard [kanar]	duck	**fraise de veau** [frɛz də vo]	crow of veal (offal)
cervelle [sɛrvɛl]	brains	**gélinotte** [ʒelinɔt]	grouse
chapon [ʃapɔ̃]	capon	**gigot** [ʒigo]	leg of lamb
chateaubriand [ʃatobrijɑ̃]	thick, succulent cut of beef	**gras-double** [gradubl]	tripe
cheval [ʃəval]	horse	**grillades** [grijad]	grilled meat
chevreau [ʃəvro]	kid	**grive** [griv]	thrush
chevreuil [ʃəvrœj]	venison	**jarret de veau** [ʒarə də vo]	knuckle of veal
civet de lièvre [sive də ljɛvr]	jugged hare	**langue** [lɑ̃g]	tongue
cochon de lait [kɔʃɔ̃ də lɛ]	suckling pig	**lapin** [lapɛ̃]	rabbit
cœur [kœr]	heart	**lièvre** [ljɛvr]	hare
côte de bœuf [kot də bœf]	rib of beef	**marcassin** [markasɛ̃]	young wild boar

magret [magʀe]	duck breast	**ragoût** [ʀagu]	stew
mouton [mutɔ̃]	mutton	**ris de veau** [ʀi də vo]	veal sweetbreads
oie [wa]	goose	**rognons** [ʀɔɲɔ̃]	kidneys
perdreau [pɛʀdʀo]	partridge	**rosbif** [ʀɔzbif]	roast beef
pieds de porc [pje də pɔʀ]	pig's trotters	**sanglier** [sãglie]	wild boar
pintade [pɛ̃tad]	guinea fowl	**saucisse** [sosis]	sausage
porc [pɔʀ]	pork	**tripes** [tʀip]	tripe
poulain [pulɛ̃]	foal (i.e. young horse)	**veau** [vo]	veal
poule (au pot) [pul o po]	fowl (boiled with vegetables)	**viande** [vjãd]	meat
poulet [pule]	chicken	**volaille** [vɔlaj]	poultry

Cooking terms

à l'anglaise [a lãglɛz]	plain boiled	**frit** [fʀi]	fried
à l'étouffée [a letufe]	cooked beneath a tight lid	**fumé** [fyme]	smoked
à la florentine [a la flɔʀãtin]	with spinach	**grillé** [gʀije]	grilled
à la lyonnaise [a la liɔnɛz]	with onions	**mijoté** [miʒɔte]	simmered
à la vapeur [a la vapœʀ]	steamed	**nappé** [nape]	coated (with sauce)
au four [o fuʀ]	baked	**poché** [pɔʃe]	poached
cru/cuit [kʀy/kɥi]	raw/cooked	**poêlé** [pwale]	pan-fried
émincé [emɛ̃se]	cut in fine slices	**râpé** [ʀape]	grated
farci [faʀsi]	stuffed	**rôti** [ʀoti]	roast

Specialities

Aligot	A thick purée of potato and cheese.
Bouillabaisse	Spicy soup containing many kinds of fish, including heads and bones.
Brandade	Creamed salt cod with potatoes.
Cassoulet	Robust dish of white beans, pork sausage and duck, which should properly be baked slowly for four days.
Charcuterie	Various pork products such as ham, pâté, terrines, sausage, and so on.
Coq au vin	Chicken cooked in red wine.
Croque-madame	Croque-monsieur with a fried egg on top.
Croque-monsieur	Toasted ham and cheese sandwich.
Fromage de tête	Brawn.
Hachis parmentier	Minced meat topped with mashed potato, similar to the shepherd's pie.
Matelote	Fish stew.
Mouclade	Mussel stew.
Petit salé	Salt pork, usually served with lentils.
Pieds (et) paquets	Stuffed mutton tripe.
Pot-au-feu	Various pieces of meat, including beef, boiled with vegetables and marrow bones.
Ratatouille	Tomatoes, courgettes, aubergines, onions, peppers, garlic, stewed together in olive oil.
Salade niçoise	Salad of lettuce, tomatoes, beans, tuna, olives, green beans, potatoes.
Steak tartare	Raw minced beef, mixed with chopped onion, parsley, capers, egg yolk and various other seasonings.
Tapenade	Paste of olives, capers and anchovies to spread on bread.
Vol-au-vent	Flaky pastry shells containing a mixture of veal or chicken, mushrooms, perhaps brains or sweetbreads, in a white sauce.

Fish and shellfish

aiglefin [egləfɛ̃]	haddock	**lamproie** [lãpʀwa]	lamprey
alose [aloz]	shad	**limande** [limãd]	dab
anguille [ãgij]	eel	**lotte** [lɔt]	monkfish
bar [baʀ]	dace, bass	**maquereau** [makʀo]	mackerel
barbue [baʀby]	brill	**merlan** [mɛʀlã]	whiting
brochet [bʀɔʃɛ]	pike	**morue** [mɔʀy]	salt cod
cabillaud [kabijo]	cod	**perche** [pɛʀʃ]	perch
carpe [kaʀp]	carp	**raie** [ʀɛ]	skate
carrelet [kaʀlɛ]	plaice	**rouget** [ʀuʒɛ]	red mullet
colin [kɔlɛ̃]	hake	**sardine** [saʀdin]	sardine
dorade [dɔʀad]	dorado	**saumon** [somɔ̃]	salmon
éperlan [epɛʀlã]	smelt	**sole** [sɔl]	sole
espadon [ɛspadɔ̃]	swordfish	**thon** [tɔ̃]	tuna
esturgeon [ɛstyʀʒɔ̃]	sturgeon	**truite** [tʀɥit]	trout
hareng [aʀã]	herring	**turbot** [tyʀbo]	turbot

Sauces

Ailloli/aïoli	A garlicky mayonnaise.
Anchoïade	Pungent purée of garlic, anchovies and parsley.
Béarnaise	Egg yolks, melted butter and herbs.
Béchamel	Melted butter, flour and milk.
Bercy	Shallots, white wine and fish stock.
Beurre noir	Browned butter.
Bordelaise	Bone marrow, red wine and herbs.

Bourguignonne	Red wine sauce flavoured with bacon, onions, mushrooms and herbs.		
Chasseur	White wine, veal stock, cognac, mushrooms and onions.		
Dijonnaise	A kind of mayonnaise made from hard-boiled egg yolks, mustard, lemon juice and oil.		
Hollandaise	Egg yolks, melted butter and vinegar.		
Maître d'hôtel	Creamed butter, parsley, chives, lemon juice.		
Mayonnaise	An emulsion of egg yolk and oil, flavoured with mustard, salt and pepper, lemon juice or vinegar.		
Mornay	White sauce flavoured with cheese.		
Ravigote	Vinaigrette with lots of herbs.		
Soubise	Lots of onions, butter, flour.		
Tartare	Mayonnaise with chopped shallots and herbs.		
Vinaigrette	Vinegar, oil, salt and pepper.		

Herbs and Spices

Herbs are used liberally in French cuisine. These are the most common.

ail [aj]	garlic	**muscade** [myskad]	nutmeg
anis [ani]	aniseed	**origan** [ɔʀigɑ̃]	oregano
cannelle [kanɛl]	cinnamon	**persil** [pɛʀsi]	parsley
cerfeuil [sɛʀfœj]	chervil	**piment** [pimɑ̃]	pimento
ciboulette [sibulɛt]	chives	**romarin** [ʀɔmaʀɛ̃]	rosemary
estragon [ɛstʀagɔ̃]	tarragon	**sauge** [soʒ]	sage
marjolaine [maʀʒɔlɛn]	marjoram	**thym** [tɛ̃]	thyme

Vegetables

Main dishes are served with rice *(riz)*, pasta *(pâtes)*, French fries *(pommes frites* or *allumettes)* and/or a vegetable.

artichaut [aʀtiʃo]	artichoke	**fèves** [fɛv]	broad beans
asperge [aspɛʀʒ]	asparagus	**haricots verts** [aʀiko vɛʀ]	runner beans
aubergine [obɛʀʒin]	aubergine	**laitue** [lety]	lettuce
betterave [bɛtʀav]	beetroot	**légume** [legym]	vegetable
brocoli [bʀɔkɔli]	broccoli	**lentilles** [lɑ̃tij]	lentils
carotte [kaʀɔt]	carrot	**mâche** [maʃ]	lamb's lettuce
céleri [selʀi]	celery	**maïs** [mais]	sweetcorn
champignon [ʃɑ̃piɲɔ̃]	mushroom	**navet** [nave]	turnip
chou [ʃu]	cabbage	**oignon** [ɔɲɔ̃]	onion
chou-fleur [ʃu flœʀ]	cauliflower	**oseille** [osɛj]	sorrel
chou rouge [ʃu ʀuʒ]	red cabbage	**petits pois** [pəti pwa]	peas
choux de Bruxelles [ʃu də bʀysɛl]	Brussels sprouts	**pissenlit** [pisɑ̃li]	dandelion
concombre [kɔ̃kɔ̃bʀ]	cucumber	**poireau** [pwaʀo]	leek
courge [kuʀʒ]	marrow	**poivron** [pwavʀɔ̃]	sweet pepper
cresson [kʀesɔ̃]	watercress	**potiron** [pɔtiʀɔ̃]	pumpkin
échalote [eʃalɔt]	shallot	**pousses de soja** [pus də sɔʒa]	beansprouts
endive [ɑ̃div]	endives	**purée** [pyʀe]	mashed potato
épinards [epinaʀ]	spinach	**radis** [ʀadi]	radish
fenouil [fənuj]	fennel	**truffes** [tʀyf]	truffles

abricot [abʀiko]	apricot	**marron** [maʀɔ̃]	chestnut
amande [amɑ̃d]	almond	**melon** [məlɔ̃]	melon
ananas [ananas]	pineapple	**mirabelle** [miʀabɛl]	small yellow plum
baies des bois [bɛ de bwa]	wild berries	**mûre** [myʀ]	blackberry
banane [banan]	banana	**myrtille** [miʀtij]	bilberry
brugnon [bʀyɲɔ̃]	nectarine	**noisette** [nwazɛt]	hazelnut
cassis [kasi]	blackcurrant	**noix** [nwa]	walnut
cerise [səʀiz]	cherry	**noix de coco** [nwa də koko]	coconut
citron [sitʀɔ̃]	lemon	**orange** [ɔʀɑ̃ʒ]	orange
citron vert [citʀɔ̃ vɛʀ]	lime	**pamplemousse** [pɑ̃pləmus]	grapefruit
coing [kwɛ̃]	quince	**pastèque** [pastɛk]	watermelon
datte [dat]	date	**pêche** [pɛʃ]	peach
figue [fig]	fig	**poire** [pwaʀ]	pear
fraise [fʀɛz]	strawberry	**pomme** [pɔm]	apple
framboise [fʀɑ̃bwaz]	raspberry	**prune** [pʀyn]	plum
fruit de la passion [fʀɥi də la pasjɔ̃]	passionfruit	**pruneau** [pʀyno]	prune
griotte [gʀiɔt]	morello cherry	**raisin** [ʀɛzɛ̃]	grapes
groseille [gʀɔsɛj]	redcurrant	**raisins de Corinthe** [ʀɛzɛ̃ də kɔʀɛ̃t]	currants
kaki [kaki]	persimmon	**raisins secs** [ʀɛzɛ̃ sɛk]	raisins
mangue [mɑ̃g]	mango	**rhubarbe** [ʀybaʀb]	rhubarb

Desserts

beignets aux pommes [bɛɲe o pɔm]	apple fritters	**massepain** [maspɛ̃]	marzipan
clafoutis [klafuti]	oven-baked cherry pudding	**merveilles** [mɛʀvɛj]	fritters
crème anglaise [kʀɛm ɑ̃glɛz]	custard	**miel** [mjɛl]	honey
crème caramel [kʀɛm kaʀamɛl]	caramel custard	**pain perdu** [pɛ̃ pɛʀdy]	French toast
		quatre-quarts [kat kaʀ]	heavy sponge cake
crème chantilly [kʀɛm ʃɑ̃tiji]	whipped cream	**Reine de Saba** [ʀɛn də saba]	chocolate cake
crêpes [kʀɛp]	pancakes	**riz au lait** [ʀi o lɛ]	rice pudding
diplomate [diplɔmat]	trifle	**sabayon** [sabajɔ̃]	syllabub
entremets [ɑ̃tʀəmɛ]	dessert	**salade de fruits** [salad də fʀɥi]	fruit salad
flan [flɑ̃]	custard	**semoule** [səmul]	semolina
gâteau de riz [gɑto də ʀi]	solid cold rice pudding	**tarte aux fruits** [taʀt o fʀɥi]	fruit tart
gâteau de Savoie [gɑto de savwa]	light sponge cake	**tôt-fait** [to fɛ]	slightly soggy sponge cake
glace [glas]	ice cream	**yaourt** [jauʀ]	yoghurt

Drinks

In France it's considered very important that you choose the right drink to go with your meal. Don't hesitate to ask the wine waiter for advice.

I'm thirsty.	**J'ai soif!** [ʒe swaf]
What do you recommend?	**Que recommandez-vous?** [kə ʀəkɔmɑ̃de vu]
I'd like a good red wine.	**J'aimerais un bon vin rouge.** [ʒeməʀɛ œ̃ bɔ̃ vɛ̃ ʀuʒ]

... white/rosé wine	**... vin blanc/vin rosé** [vɛ̃ blɑ̃] [vɛ̃ ʀɔze]
... champagne	**... champagne** [ʃɑ̃paɲ]
a glass	**un verre** [œ̃ vɛʀ]
a bottle	**une bouteille** [yn butɛj]
a half-bottle	**une demi-bouteille** [yn dəmi butɛj]
Another bottle, please.	**Une deuxième bouteille, s'il vous plaît.** [yn døzjɛm butɛj silvuplɛ]
pre-dinner drink	**un apéritif** [œ̃naperitif]
after-dinner drink	**un digestif** [œ̃ diʒɛstif]
port	**du porto** [dy pɔʀto]
sherry	**du vin de Xérès, du sherry** [dy vɛ̃ də kseʀɛs/dy ʃeʀi]
mineral water...	**de l'eau minérale...** [də lo mineʀal]
... flat/fizzy	**... plate/gazeuse** [plat] [gazøz]
a jug of plain (tap) water	**une carafe d'eau** [yn kaʀaf do]
alcoholic drink	**une boisson alcoolisée** [yn bwasɔ̃ alkɔlize]
soft drink	**une boisson non alcoolisée** [yn bwasɔ̃ nɔnalkɔlize]
fizzy soft drink	**un soda** [œ̃ sɔda]

BISTROT BEHAVIOUR

When you go into a bistrot you can either sit down at a table and wait until someone comes to serve you, or stand at the counter and order from the barman. With each round you order, you will be given a little chit. When you want to pay, call the waiter and he will come and add everything up. The tip is included, but you can always leave a few extra coins if you're happy with the service.

Let's go for a drink.	**Allons boire un verre.** [alɔ̃ bwaʀ œ̃ vɛʀ]
What would you like?	**Qu'est-ce que vous prenez?** [kɛskə vu pʀəne]
A glass of beer, please.	**Une bière, s'il vous plaît.** [yn bjɛʀ silvuplɛ]
Cheers!	**Santé!** [sɑ̃te]
Keep the change.	**Gardez la monnaie.** [gaʀde la mɔnɛ]

draught beer	**bière à la pression** [bjɛʀ a la pʀɛsjɔ̃]	syrup	**un sirop de grenadine** [œ̃ siʀo də gʀənadin]
lager	**bière blonde** [bjɛʀ blɔ̃d]	mint cordial	**une menthe à l'eau** [yn mɑ̃talo]
stout	**bière brune** [bjɛʀ bʀyn]		
shandy	**un panaché** [œ̃ panaʃe]	a glass of milk	**un verre de lait** [œ̃ vɛʀ də lɛ]
alcohol-free beer	**bière sans alcool** [bjɛʀ sɑ̃zalcɔl]	hot/cold chocolate	**chocolat chaud/froid** [ʃɔkola ʃo/fʀwa]
cider	**du cidre** [dy sidʀ]	tea	**un thé** [œ̃ te]
orange juice	**un jus d'orange** [œ̃ ʒy dɔʀɑ̃ʒ]	tea with lemon	**thé citron** [te sitʀɔ̃]
lemonade	**une limonade** [yn limɔnad]	black tea	**un thé nature** [œ̃ te natyʀ]
fresh lemon juice	**un citron pressé** [œ̃ sitʀɔ̃ pʀese]	mint tea	**thé de menthe** [te də mɑ̃t]

shopping

Whether you are interested in food, fashion or furniture, you'll find that French shops are absolutely fascinating. The prices are not particularly cheap, but you're bound to find bargains if you look properly.

The huge *supermarchés* and *hypermarchés* clustered in the industrial zones outside the big towns are great value for a wide selection of goods from food and wine to kitchen china, toiletries, stationery and household gadgets.

Flea markets and *brocantes* (junk shops) can be good hunting grounds for bric-à-brac, but many of them tend to be touristy. Here, you can try your hand at bargaining.

Department stores open Mon–Sat 9 or 10 a.m.–6.30 or 7.30 p.m., and most have late opening one night a week. Boutiques may open as late as 11 a.m. or noon—introduction of the 35-hour week has played havoc with opening times.

SHOPS AND BOUTIQUES

The sales (*soldes*) begin as soon as Christmas is over, as the stores clear their shelves to make way for summer stock. Then it all starts again in July. Note that the term *En promotion* refers to goods that have been specially bulk-bought to sell at a low price.

Let's go shopping!	**On va faire des achats?** [ɔ̃ va fɛʀ dezaʃa]
I fancy doing some window shopping!	**J'ai envie de faire du lèche-vitrine!** [ʒe ɑ̃vi də fɛʀ dy lɛʃ vitʀin]
What time do the shops open/close?	**A quelle heure ouvrent/ferment les boutiques?** [a kɛl œʀ uvʀ/fɛʀm le butik]
open/closed	**ouvert/fermé** [uvɛʀ] [fɛʀme]
When's market day?	**Quel est le jour de marché?** [kɛl ɛ lə juʀ də maʀʃe]
I'm looking for a/an...	**Je cherche...** [ʒə ʃɛʀʃ]

antique dealers	**un antiquaire** [œ̃ nɑ̃tikɛʀ]	jewellers	**une bijouterie** [yn biʒutʀi]
bookshop	**une librairie** [yn libʀeʀi]	newsagents	**un kiosque** [œ̃ kiɔsk]
camera shop	**un magasin de photo** [œ̃ magazɛ̃ də fɔto]	record shop	**un disquaire** [œ̃ diskɛʀ]
craft shop	**un magasin d'artisanat** [œ̃ magazɛ̃ daʀtizanat]	shoe shop	**un magasin de chaussures** [œ̃ magazɛ̃ də ʃosyʀ]
flea market	**un marché aux puces** [œ̃ maʀʃe o pys]	stationers	**une papeterie** [yn papɛtʀi]
		toy shop	**un magasin de jouets** [œ̃ magazɛ̃ də jue]
florist	**un fleuriste** [œ̃ flœʀist]		

CHOOSING

In most shops you can browse without anybody fussing around you. But the sales assistants (*vendeur* or *vendeuse*) will be of great help if you want to know if something suits you. And if you tell them it's a present (*c'est un cadeau*), they will wrap it beautifully.

Can I look around?	**Est-ce que je peux jeter un coup d'œil?** [εskə ʒə pø jəte œ̃ ku dœj]
I'm just looking.	**Je ne fais que regarder.** [ʒə nə fɛ kə ʀəgaʀde]
I'd like to try this on.	**Je voudrais essayer ça.** [ʒə vudʀɛ esɛje sa]
Where are the changing rooms?	**Où sont les cabines d'essayage?** [u sɔ̃ le kabin dɛsɛjaʒ]
It's too...	**C'est trop...** [sɛ tʀo]
... big/small/tight	**... grand/petit/serré** [gʀɑ̃] [pəti] [sɛʀe]
Do you have it in other colours?	**L'avez-vous dans d'autres coloris?** [lave vu dɑ̃ dotʀ kɔlɔʀi]
Can you put it aside for me?	**Pouvez-vous me le mettre de côté?** [puve vu mə lə mɛtʀ də kote]
How much is it?	**Combien ça coûte?** [kɔ̃bjɛ̃ sa kut]
Where's the cash desk?	**Où est la caisse?** [u ɛ la kɛs]
Do you accept credit cards?	**Acceptez-vous les cartes de crédit?** [aksɛpte vu le kaʀt də kʀedi]
Can I have a receipt?	**Est-ce que je peux avoir le ticket de caisse?** [εskə ʒə pø avwaʀ lə tike də kɛs]

FASHION

The clothes are fabulous, but make sure you try everything on, as the sizes may be smaller than you imagine.

I'm looking for a/an/some...   Je cherche...
[ʒə ʃɛrʃ]

bathing costume	**un maillot de bain** [œ̃ majo də bɛ̃]	shirt	**une chemise** [yn ʃəmiz]
blouse	**un chemisier** [œ̃ ʃəmizje]	shorts	**un short** [œ̃ ʃɔrt]
bra	**un soutien-gorge** [œ̃ sutjɛ̃gɔrʒ]	skirt	**une jupe** [yn ʒyp]
		socks	**des chaussettes** [de ʃosɛt]
coat	**un manteau** [œ̃ mɑ̃to]	suit (for a man)	**un complet** [œ̃ kɔ̃plɛ]
dress	**une robe** [yn rɔb]	suit (for a women)	**un tailleur** [œ̃ tajœr]
jacket	**une veste** [yn vɛst]	sweater	**un pull** [œ̃ pyl]
jeans	**un jean** [œ̃ dʒin]	trousers	**un pantalon** [œ̃ pɑ̃talɔ̃]

Costume jewellery (*les bijoux fantaisie*) is great fun and not too expensive. And you'll need a little scarf or hat to make your new outfit truly *chic*. In a department store, you'll find all these in the *rayon des colifichets*.

bracelet	**un bracelet** [œ̃ brasle]	necklace	**un collier** [œ̃ kɔlje]
brooch	**une broche** [yn brɔʃ]	pendant	**un pendentif** [œ̃ pɑ̃dɑ̃tif]
earrings	**des boucles d'oreilles** [de bukl dɔrej]	ring	**une bague** [yn bag]
		scarf	**une écharpe** [yn eʃarp]
hat	**un chapeau** [œ̃ ʃapo]	tie	**une cravate** [yn kravat]
headsquare	**un foulard** [œ̃ fulɑr]	watch	**une montre** [yn mɔ̃tr]

You'll need to know the names of colours, even if shopping isn't your thing. These are the main shades:

beige	**beige** [bɛʒ]	orange	**orange** [ɔʀɑ̃ʒ]
black	**noir** [nwaʀ]	pink	**rose** [ʀoz]
blue	**bleu** [blø]	purple	**violet** [vjɔle]
brown	**brun** [bʀœ̃]	red	**rouge** [ʀuʒ]
green	**vert** [vɛʀ]	sky blue	**bleu ciel** [blø sjɛl]
grey	**gris** [gʀi]	turquoise	**turquoise** [tyʀkwaz]
maroon	**bordeaux** [bɔʀdo]	white	**blanc** [blɑ̃]
navy blue	**bleu marine** [blø maʀin]	yellow	**jaune** [ʒon]

light	**clair** [klɛʀ]	bright	**lumineux** [lyminø]
dark	**foncé** [fɔ̃se]	pale	**pâle** [pɑl]
deep	**intense** [ɛ̃tɑ̃s]	transparent	**transparent** [tʀɑ̃spaʀɑ̃]

When you buy clothes, check the labels to see what they are made of. Man-made fibres generally have the same names in French as in English—nylon, polyester, polyamide, etc.

cotton	**le coton** [lə kɔtɔ̃]	silk	**la soie** [la swa]
lace	**la dentelle** [la dɑ̃tɛl]	taffeta	**le taffetas** [lə tafta]
linen	**le lin** [lə lɛ̃]	velvet	**le velours** [lə vəluʀ]
satin	**le satin** [lə satɛ̃]	wool	**la laine** [la lɛn]

75

Shoe sizes vary, depending on what country they were made in. You can always ask the sales assistant to measure your foot if you're not sure of your size.

I'd like a pair of...	**J'aimerais une paire de...** [jɛməʀɛ yn pɛʀ də]
... boots	**... bottes** [bɔt]
... high-heeled shoes	**... chaussures à talons** [ʃosyʀ a talɔ̃]
... hiking boots	**... chaussures de marche** [ʃosyʀ də maʀʃ]
... sandals	**... sandales** [sɑ̃dal]
... slippers	**... pantoufles** [pɑ̃tufl]
... trainers	**... baskets** [baskɛt]
I take size 39.	**Je chausse du 39.** [ʒə ʃos dy tʀɑ̃tnœf]
I don't know the sizes you use.	**Je ne connais pas les tailles d'ici.** [ʒə nə kɔnɛ pa lə taj disi]
Is it real leather?	**Est-ce du cuir véritable?** [ɛs dy kɥiʀ veʀitabl]

canvas	**la toile** [la twal]	suede	**le daim** [lə dɛ̃]
leather	**le cuir** [lə kɥiʀ]	heel	**le talon** [lə talɔ̃]
plastic	**le plastique** [lə plastik]	sole	**la semelle** [la səmɛl]
rubber	**le caoutchouc** [lə kautʃu]	uppers	**l'empeigne** [lɑ̃pɛɲ]

I'd like to try the other foot.	**J'aimerais essayer l'autre pied.** [ʒɛmərɛ ɛsɛje lotr pje]		
Have you a shoe-horn?	**Avez-vous un chausse-pieds?** [ave vu œ̃ ʃos pje]		
Do you have the same in the next size up/down?	**Avez-vous les mêmes dans une pointure de plus/moins?** [ave vu le mɛm dã yn pwɛ̃tyr də plys/mwɛ̃]		
They are too wide/narrow.	**Elles sont trop larges/étroites.** [ɛl sɔ̃ tro larʒ/etrwat]		
Could you stretch them a bit?	**Pourriez-vous les élargir un peu?** [purie vu lezelarʒir œ̃ pø]		
I need a pair of inner soles.	**Il me faudrait des semelles.** [il mə fodrɛ de səmɛl]		
They are very comfortable.	**Elles sont très confortables.** [ɛl sɔ̃ trɛ kɔ̃fɔrtabl]		
I'll take them.	**Je les prends.** [ʒə le prã]		
Could you waterproof them?	**Pourriez-vous les imperméabiliser?** [purie vu lezɛ̃permeabilize]		
I need some shoe polish.	**J'ai besoin de cirage.** [ʒe bəzwɛ̃ də siraʒ]		

Now you have your shoes, are you sure you don't need a bag to go with them?

Do you have any bags to match?	**Avez-vous des sacs assortis?** [ave vu de sak asɔrti]

belt	**une ceinture** [yn sɛ̃tyr]	purse	**un porte-monnaie** [œ̃ pɔrt mɔnɛ]
handbag	**un sac à main** [œ̃ sak a mɛ̃]	wallet	**un portefeuille** [œ̃ pɔrtəfœj]

77

AT THE HAIRDRESSER'S

There's nothing like a séance in a French *salon de coiffure* to make you feel on top of the world. In French, hair (*les cheveux*) is plural.

Do you know a good hairdresser?	**Connaissez-vous un bon coiffeur?** [kɔnɛse vu œ̃ bɔ̃ kwafœʀ]
Can you fit me in now?	**Pouvez-vous me prendre sans rendez-vous?** [puve vu mə pʀɑ̃dʀ sɑ̃ ʀɑ̃devu]
Could I call in a bit later?	**Est-ce que je peux passer un peu plus tard?** [ɛskə ʒə pø pase œ̃ pø ply taʀ]
I'd like to make an appointment for tomorrow.	**Je voudrais prendre un rendez-vous pour demain.** [ʒə vudʀɛ pʀɑ̃dʀ œ̃ ʀɑ̃devu puʀ dəmɛ̃]
I'd like a...	**J'aimerais...** [ʒɛməʀɛ]
... cut and blow-dry	**... une coupe et brushing** [yn kup ɛ bʀœʃiŋ]
... shampoo and set	**... une mise en plis** [yn mizɑ̃ pli]
... perm	**... une permanente** [yn pɛʀmanɑ̃t]
Could you...	**Pourriez-vous...** [puʀie vu]
... trim my fringe	**... couper la frange** [kupe la fʀɑ̃ʒ]
... trim the ends	**... couper les pointes** [kupe le pwɛ̃t]
... cut it short	**... les couper court** [le kupe kuʀ]
... put in some highlights	**... faire des mèches** [fɛʀ de mɛʃ]

... change the colour	**... changer la couleur** [ʃɑ̃ʒe la kulœʀ]
My hair is...	**J'ai les cheveux...** [ʒe le ʃəvø]
... dry/greasy/normal/fragile	**...secs/gras/normaux/cassants** [sɛk] [gʀa] [nɔʀmo] [kasɑ̃]
I'd prefer you to use...	**Je préfère si vous les coupez...** [ʒə pʀefeʀ si vu le kupe]
... scissors	**... aux ciseaux** [o sizo]
... clippers	**... à la tondeuse** [a la tɔ̃døz]
... a razor	**... au rasoir** [o ʀazwaʀ]
Cut more off...	**Coupez un peu plus...** [kupe œ̃ pø plys]
... the back	**... derrière** [dɛʀyɛʀ]
... the front	**... devant** [dəvɑ̃]
... the sides	**... sur les côtés** [syʀ le kote]
Not too short.	**Pas trop court.** [pa tʀo kuʀ]
Could you give me a manicure?	**Pourriez-vous me faire une manucure?** [puʀie vu mə fɛʀ yn manykyʀ]
Could you trim my beard?	**Pouvez-vous me couper la barbe?** [puve vu mə kupe la baʀb]
Could you give me a shave?	**Pouvez-vous me raser la barbe?** [puve vu mə ʀaze la baʀb]
Shave off my moustache.	**Rasez-moi la moustache.** [ʀaze mwa la mustaʃ]

PHOTOGRAPHY

It's just typical. You're on holiday, the weather is fantastic, the colours are perfect and the scenery beautiful, and something's gone wrong with your camera...

I have a problem with my camera.	**J'ai un problème avec mon appareil photo.** [ʒe œ̃ pʀɔblɛm avɛk mɔ̃ apaʀɛj fɔto]
Can it be repaired?	**Peut-on le réparer?** [pøtɔ̃ lə ʀepaʀe]
The batteries are flat.	**Les piles sont usées.** [le pil sɔ̃ yze]
I'd like to buy a...	**J'aimerais acheter...** [ʒɛməʀɛ aʃte]
... film	**... un film, une pellicule** [œ̃ film] [yn pɛlikyl]
... cassette	**... une cassette** [yn kasɛt]
I'd like to develop some...	**J'aimerais faire développer des...** [ʒɛməʀɛ fɛʀ devəlɔpe de]
... slides/photos	**... diapositives/photos** [djapozitiv] [fɔto]
on glossy/matt paper	**sur papier brillant/mat** [syʀ papje bʀijɑ̃/mat]
Could I have the pictures on a CD-rom?	**Est-il possible d'avoir les photos sur CD-ROM?** [ɛtil pɔsibl davwaʀ le fɔto syʀ sedeʀɔm]
I'd like prints of digital images.	**J'aimerais un tirage photo d'images numériques.** [ʒɛməʀɛ œ̃ tiʀaʒ fɔto dimaʒ nymeʀik]
When will they be ready?	**Ce sera prêt quand?** [sə səʀa pʀɛ kɑ̃]

Leisure

One thing is certain, you'll never be bored. Whether you like sport or culture, prefer classical concerts or techno music, you'll find plenty to keep you busy.

France is a vast and varied country, and every region is bursting with historical monuments, churches and cathedrals, palaces and châteaux. If it rains, you can nip into a museum or art gallery for an hour or so. You can listen to an opera in a Roman arena, sail along the canals of Burgundy or go painting in Provence. The tourist offices are full of ideas, mapping out routes on various themes such as the Cathar castles, cheese-making in Normandy or volcanoes in Auvergne. Every day, wherever you are, there'll be a local market full of noise and colour, a village square where the men play boules, a friendly bistrot where you can sit outside on the pavement, sip a *pastis* and watch the world go by.

SIGHTSEEING

Before you leave home, gather all the information you can from the government tourist office (*Maison de la France*), web site www.franceguide.com or for Paris, www.paris.touristoffice.com. And you'll find a helpful local office, the *Syndicat d'Initiative,* in every other town.

Where is the tourist office?	**Où est l'Office du Tourisme?** [u ε lɔfis dy turism]
Could you give me a city map?	**Pourriez-vous me donner un plan de la ville?** [purie vu mə dɔne œ̃ plã də la vil]
I'd like some information...	**J'aimerais des renseignements...** [ʒɛmərɛ de rãsɛɲəmã]
... about guided tours of the city	**... sur les visites guidées de la ville** [syr le vizit gide də la vil]
... on the monuments open for visits	**... sur les monuments à voir** [syr le mɔnymã a vwar]
... on the museums' opening times	**... sur les heures d'ouverture des musées** [syr lezœr duvɛrtyr de myze]
Can you give me some brochures?	**Avez-vous des brochures à me donner?** [ave vu de brɔʃyr a mə dɔne]
Is there anything interesting to see?	**Y a-t-il quelque chose d'intéressant à voir?** [jatil kɛlkə ʃoz dɛ̃teresã a vwar]
What else is there to see in the region?	**Qu'est-ce qu'il y a encore à voir dans la région?** [keskil ja ãkɔr a vwar dã la reʒjɔ̃]
Are there any organized excursions?	**Y a-t-il des excursions?** [jatil dez ekskyrsjɔ̃]

(botanic) garden	**un jardin (botanique)** [œ̃ ʒaʀdɛ̃ bɔtanik]	fortress	**une forteresse** [yn fɔʀtəʀɛs]
(theme) park	**un parc (à thèmes)** [œ̃ paʀk a tɛm]	fountain display	**des jeux d'eau** [de ʒø do]
abbey	**une abbaye** [yn abɛj]	historic site	**un site historique** [œ̃ sit istɔʀik]
archaeological site	**un site archéologique** [œ̃ sit aʀkeɔlɔʒik]	manor	**un manoir** [œ̃ manwaʀ]
		mill	**un moulin** [œ̃ mulɛ̃]
arena	**des arènes** [dezaʀɛn]	monastery	**un monastère** [œ̃ mɔnastɛʀ]
art gallery	**une galerie d'art** [yn galʀi daʀ]	museum	**un musée** [œ̃ myze]
		nature reserve	**une réserve naturelle** [yn ʀezɛʀv natyʀɛl]
battlefield	**un champ de bataille** [œ̃ ʃɑ̃ də bataj]		
birthplace	**un lieu de naissance** [œ̃ ljø də nɛsɑ̃s]	palace	**un palais** [œ̃ palɛ]
		priory	**un prieuré** [œ̃ pʀiœʀe]
castle	**un château** [œ̃ ʃato]	ramparts	**les remparts** [le ʀɑ̃paʀ]
cathedral	**une cathédrale** [yn katedʀal]	rock paintings	**des peintures rupestres** [de pɛ̃tyʀ ʀypɛstʀ]
cave	**une grotte** [yn gʀɔt]		
chapel	**une chapelle** [yn ʃapɛl]	ruins	**des ruines** [de ʀɥin]
church	**une église** [yn egliz]	sound and light	**un son et lumière** [œ̃ sɔ̃ e lymjɛʀ]
cliff	**une falaise** [yn falɛz]		
cloister	**un cloître** [œ̃ klwatʀ]	temple	**un temple** [œ̃ tɑ̃pl]
convent	**un couvent** [œ̃ kuvɑ̃]	theatre	**un théâtre** [œ̃ teatʀ]
ducal palace	**un palais ducal** [œ̃ palɛ dykal]	tower	**une tour** [yn tuʀ]
fishing harbour	**un port de pêche** [œ̃ pɔʀ də pɛʃ]	viewpoint	**un belvédère** [œ̃ bɛlvedɛʀ]

83

The best place to learn about the place your staying in is the local museum. Many have free admission (*entrée gratuite*).

How much is it to get in?	**Combien coûte l'entrée?** [kɔ̃bjɛ̃ kut lɑ̃tre]
Is photography allowed?	**Est-ce qu'on peut prendre des photos?** [ɛskɔ̃ pø prɑ̃dr de fɔto]
Have you a guide in English?	**Avez-vous un guide du musée en anglais?** [ave vu œ̃ gid dy myze ɑ̃nɑ̃glɛ]
What time is the next guided tour?	**A quelle heure est la prochaine visite guidée?** [a kɛl œr ɛ la prɔʃen vizit gide]
What's the theme of...	**Quel est le sujet...** [kɛl ɛ lə syʒe]
... the permanent collections?	**...des collections permanentes?** [de kɔlɛksjɔ̃ pɛrmanɑ̃t]
... the temporary exhibition ?	**... de l'exposition temporaire?** [də lɛkspozisjɔ̃ tɑ̃pɔrɛr]

ceramics	**la céramique** [la seramik]	photography	**la photographie** [la fɔtɔgrafi]
enamel	**l'émail** [lemaj]	sculpture	**la sculpture** [la skyltyr]
engraving	**la gravure** [la gravyr]	silver	**l'argent** [larʒɑ̃]
glass	**le verre** [lə vɛr]	stained-glass	**le vitrail** [lə vitraj]
gold	**l'or** [lɔr]	stone	**la pierre** [la pjɛr]
marble	**le marbre** [lə marbr]	tapestry	**la tapisserie** [la tapisri]
mosaics	**les mosaïques** [le mɔzaik]	watercolour	**l'aquarelle** [lakwarɛl]
painting	**la peinture** [la pɛ̃tyr]	wood	**le bois** [lə bwa]

ENTERTAINMENT

Jazz and film festivals, opera, dance, theatre, cinema, there's bound to be something that tickles your taste buds.

What's on tonight?	**Qu'est-ce qu'il y a ce soir?** [kɛskil ja sə swaʀ]
Where can we buy tickets?	**Où est-ce qu'on achète les billets?** [u ɛskɔ̃naʃɛt le bije]
Are there any seats left?	**Est-ce qu'il reste des places?** [ɛskil ʀɛst de plas]
I'd like...	**J'aimerais...** [ʒɛməʀɛ]
... the cheapest seats	**... les places les moins chères** [le plas le mwɛ̃ ʃɛʀ]
... the best seats	**... les meilleures places** [le mɛjœʀ plas]
There are two of us.	**Nous sommes deux.** [nu sɔm dø]
Are there any reductions for students?	**Est-ce qu'il y a des rabais pour les étudiants?** [ɛskil ja de ʀabɛ puʀ lezetydjɑ̃]
What time does the performance start?	**A quelle heure débute la représentation?** [a kel œʀ debyt la ʀəpʀezɑ̃tasjɔ̃]

balcony	**le balcon** [lə balkɔ̃]	row	**le rang** [lə ʀɑ̃]
booking	**la réservation** [la ʀezɛʀvasjɔ̃]	seat	**le siège** [lə sjɛʒ]
interval	**l'entracte** [lɑ̃tʀakt]	show	**le spectacle** [lə spɛktakl]
pit	**le parterre** [lə paʀtɛʀ]	ticket office	**le guichet** [lə giʃe]
programme	**le programme** [lə pʀogʀam]	usherette	**l'ouvreuse** [luvʀøz]

If you're in France on the 14th July, don't miss the *bal populaire*—everyone from toddlers to grannies dancing in the streets. The French love old-fashioned dancing, but there are plenty of discos, too.

What shall we do tonight?	**Qu'est-ce qu'on va faire ce soir?** [kɛskɔ̃ va fɛʀ sə swaʀ]
I've been invited to a party, would you like to come?	**Je suis invité(e) à une soirée; veux-tu m'accompagner?** [ʒə sɥizɛ̃vite a yn swaʀe vø ty makɔ̃paɲe]
Do you prefer dancing or listening to music?	**Est-ce que tu préfères danser ou écouter de la musique?** [ɛskə ty pʀefɛʀ dɑ̃se u ekute də la myzik]
Let's go to a...	**Allons dans...** [alɔ̃ dɑ̃]
... bar	**... un bar** [œ̃ baʀ]
... casino	**... un casino** [œ̃ kazino]
... concert hall	**... une salle de concerts** [yn sal də kɔ̃sɛʀ]
... disco	**... une discothèque** [yn diskɔtɛk]
... nightclub	**... une boîte de nuit** [yn bwat də nɥi]
We could meet at the station at 9 p.m.	**On peut se donner rendez-vous devant la gare à 21 heures.** [ɔ̃ pø sə dɔne ʀɑ̃devu dəvɑ̃ la gaʀ a vɛ̃teyn œʀ]
What time do people usually start coming?	**A quelle heure viennent les gens d'habitude?** [a kɛl œʀ vjɛn le ʒɑ̃ dabityd]

What kind of music do they play?	**Quel genre de musique est-ce qu'ils passent?** [kel ʒɑ̃r də myzik ɛskil pas]	
I'm over 18.	**J'ai plus de 18 ans.** [ʒe ply də dizɥitɑ̃]	
What would you like to drink?	**Qu'est-ce que tu aimerais boire?** [kɛskə ty ɛmərɛ bwar]	
The first drink is free.	**La première boisson est gratuite.** [la prəmjɛr bwasɔ̃ ɛ gratɥit]	
Will you dance with me?	**Tu danses avec moi?** [ty dɑ̃s avɛk mwa]	
I can't dance!	**Je ne sais pas danser!** [ʒə nə sɛ pa dɑ̃se]	
Are you trying to pick me up?	**Tu essaies de me draguer?** [ty ɛsej də mə drage]	
I'm with someone.	**Je suis accompagné(e).** [ʒə sɥizakɔ̃paɲe]	
I've had a really good time.	**J'ai passé une très bonne soirée.** [ʒe pase yn trɛ bɔn sware]	
It was great fun.	**Je me suis vraiment amusé(e).** [ʒə mə sɥi vremɑ̃ amyze]	
Thanks for the invitation.	**Merci pour l'invitation!** [mɛrsi pur lɛ̃vitasjɔ̃]	
Could you take me home?	**Tu pourrais me raccompagner?** [ty purɛ mə rakɔ̃paɲe]	

bouncers	**videurs** [vidœr]	dance floor	**piste** [pist]	
cloakroom	**vestiaire** [vɛstjɛr]	gay club	**club gay** [klœb ge]	
cover charge	**couvert** [kuvɛr]	theme night	**soirée à thèmes** [sware a tɛm]	

SPORT

There's no excuse for not keeping fit! And after all that good food and wine, you'll need a bit of exercise.

I'd like to go diving.	**J'aimerais faire de la plongée.** [ʒɛmərɛ fɛr də la plɔ̃ʒe]
Where can I rent the equipment?	**Où est-ce que je peux louer le matériel nécessaire?** [u ɛskə ʒə pø lue lə materjɛl nesɛsɛr]
Where can we play golf/tennis?	**Où est-ce qu'on peut jouer au golf/tennis?** [u ɛskɔ̃ pø ʒue o gɔlf/tɛnis]
Is there a football/rugby match?	**Est-ce qu'il y a un match de foot/de rugby?** [eskil ja œ̃ matʃ də fut/də ʀygbi]
Where can we go pot-holing?	**Où est-ce qu'on peut faire de la spéléologie?** [u ɛskɔ̃ pø fɛr də la speleɔlɔʒi]

climbing	**de la grimpe** [də la grɛ̃p]	rock-climbing	**de l'escalade** [də lɛskalad]
cross-country skiing	**du ski de fond** [dy ski də fɔ̃]	rowing	**de l'aviron** [də lavirɔ̃]
cycling	**du vélo** [dy velo]	running	**de la course à pied** [də la kurs a pje]
fishing	**de la pêche** [de la pɛʃ]		
hang-gliding	**du deltaplane** [dy dɛltaplan]	sailing	**de la voile** [də la vwal]
hiking	**de la randonnée** [də la rɑ̃dɔne]	skiing	**du ski** [dy ski]
horse-riding	**de l'équitation** [də lekitasjɔ̃]	swimming	**de la natation** [də la natasjɔ̃]
in-line skating	**du roller** [dy rɔlɛr]	water-skiing	**du ski nautique** [dy ski notik]
mountain-climbing	**de l'alpinisme** [də lalpinism]	windsurfing	**de la planche à voile** [də la plɑ̃ʃ a vwal]
paragliding	**du parapente** [dy parapɑ̃t]		

Health

It can just take an infected mosquito bite to ruin a holiday, though the biggest problems you're likely to encounter are generally caused by too much sun or too much food.

The local *pharmacies* (always signposted by a green cross) will always help you out with over-the-counter remedies; if you're suffering from something more serious they will advise a doctor (*médecin*). In the main cities, you should be able to find a doctor who speaks English, but in the countryside you may have to rely on sign language. In every town there is a duty pharmacy which stays open outside normal working hours; the address is displayed in pharmacy windows, or ask the police.

Before you leave home, get hold of an E111 form (eventually to be replaced by a European health card) which will cover you for medical expenses while in France. Make sure you keep any receipts.

CONSULTING A DOCTOR

Once you've found the doctor's surgery (*cabinet médical*), you will have to explain what's wrong with you. Here are a few basic phrases; if you have a pain somewhere, just point to the spot.

I need to see a doctor.	**Je dois consulter un médecin.** [ʒə dwa kɔ̃sylte œ̃ medsɛ̃]
Can you give me the address?	**Pourriez-vous me donner l'adresse?** [puʀje vu mə dɔne ladʀɛs]
I have an appointment with Dr Blanc.	**J'ai rendez-vous avec le docteur Blanc.** [ʒe ʀɑ̃devu avɛk lə dɔktœʀ blɑ̃]

Conversation with the doctor

Do you smoke?	**Est-ce que vous fumez?** [ɛskə vu fyme]
Are you taking medication?	**Est-ce que vous prenez des médicaments?** [ɛskə vu pʀəne de medikamɑ̃]
Are you on the pill?	**Est-ce que vous prenez la pilule contraceptive?** [ɛskə vu pʀəne la pilyl kɔ̃tʀasɛptiv]
Are you pregnant?	**Etes-vous enceinte?** [ɛt vu ɑ̃sɛ̃t]
Have you any allergies?	**Avez-vous des allergies?** [ave vu dezalɛʀʒi]
Have you had any other illnesses?	**Est-ce que vous avez eu d'autres maladies auparavant?** [ɛskə vuzave y dotʀ maladi opaʀavɑ̃]
I have diabetes/epilepsy.	**Je suis diabétique/épileptique.** [ʒə sɥi djabetik/epilɛptik]

I'm allergic to gluten.	**Je suis allergique au gluten.** [ʒə sɥizalɛrʒik o glytɛn]		
I'm HIV positive.	**Je suis séropositif/-ve.** [ʒə sɥi seropɔzitif/v]		
I don't feel well.	**Je ne me sens pas bien.** [ʒə nə mə sã pa bjɛ̃]		
I have a temperature.	**J'ai de la fièvre.** [ʒe də la fjɛvR]		
I feel sick.	**J'ai la nausée.** [ʒe la noze]		
I have cramp.	**J'ai des crampes.** [ʒe de kRãp]		
I'm shivering.	**J'ai des frissons.** [ʒe de fRisɔ̃]		
I have diarrhoea.	**J'ai la diarrhée.** [ʒe la djaRe]		
I'm constipated.	**Je suis constipé(e).** [ʒə sɥi kɔ̃stipe]		
I've been sick.	**J'ai vomi.** [ʒe vomi]		
I can't breathe.	**J'ai de la peine à respirer.** [ʒe də la pɛn a RɛspiRe]		
I have an asthma attack.	**J'ai une crise d'asthme.** [ʒe yn kRiz dasm]		
It hurts here...	**J'ai mal ici...** [ʒe mal isi]		

bladder	**vessie** [vɛsi]	kidney	**rein** [Rɛ̃]
ear	**oreille** [ɔRɛj]	liver	**foie** [fwa]
head	**tête** [tɛt]	lungs	**poumons** [pumɔ̃]
heart	**cœur** [kœR]	stomach	**ventre** [vãtR]
intestines	**intestin** [ɛ̃tɛstɛ̃]	throat	**gorge** [gɔRʒ]

The doctor's examination

Get undressed down to your waist.	**Déshabillez-vous jusqu'à la ceinture.** [dezabije vu ʒuska la sɛ̃tyʀ]
Lie down, please.	**Allongez-vous, s'il vous plaît.** [alɔ̃ʒe vu silvuplɛ]
Where does it hurt?	**Où est-ce que vous avez mal?** [u ɛskə vuz ave mal]
Does it hurt here?	**Est-ce que vous avez mal ici?** [ɛskə vuzave mal isi]
Please cough.	**Toussez, s'il vous plaît.** [tuse silvuplɛ]
I'm going to take a blood sample.	**Je vais vous faire une prise de sang.** [ʒə vɛ vu fɛʀ yn pʀiz də sɑ̃]
I'm going to take your temperature.	**Je vais prendre votre température.** [ʒə vɛ pʀɑ̃dʀ vɔtʀ tɑ̃peʀatyʀ]
I'm going to measure your blood pressure.	**Je vais mesurer votre tension.** [ʒə vɛ məzyʀe vɔtʀ tɑ̃sjɔ̃]
Your blood pressure is too high/low.	**Vous faites de l'hypertension/ l'hypotension.** [vu fɛt de lipɛʀtɑ̃sjɔ̃/lipotɑ̃sjɔ̃]
I need a specimen of your urine/stools.	**J'ai besoin d'une analyse d'urine/des selles.** [ʒə bəzwɛ̃ dyn analiz dyʀin/ de sɛl]
I'll have to do an X-ray.	**Je dois vous faire une radiographie.** [ʒə dwa vu fɛʀ yn ʀadjogʀafi]
You'll have to see a specialist.	**Il faudra voir un spécialiste.** [il fodʀa vwaʀ œ̃ spesjalist]
Don't worry, it's not serious.	**Ne vous inquiétez pas, ce n'est rien de grave.** [nə vuz ɛ̃kjete pa sə nɛ ʀjɛ̃ də gʀav]

The diagnosis

You have indigestion.	**Vous avez fait une indigestion.** [vuzave fɛ yn ɛ̃diʒɛstjɔ̃]
It's food poisoning.	**C'est une intoxication alimentaire.** [sɛtyn ɛ̃tɔksikasjɔ̃ alimɑ̃tɛʀ]
You have...	**Vous avez...** [vuz ave]

appendicitis	**l'appendicite** [lapɛ̃disit]	gastritis	**une gastrite** [yn gastʀit]
a cold	**un rhume** [ɑ̃ ʀym]	otitis	**une otite** [yn ɔtit]
cystitis	**une cystite** [yn sistit]	pneumonia	**une pneumonie** [yn pnømɔni]
flu	**la grippe** [la gʀip]	tonsillitis	**une angine** [yn ɑ̃gin]

In case of accident, or something really serious, you'd better head straight for the emergency department (*service des urgences*) of the nearest hospital, or call the SAMU who will send a doctor to wherever you are staying.

Call an ambulance!	**Appelez une ambulance!** [apəle yn ɑ̃bylɑ̃s]
I have to go to hospital.	**Je dois me rendre à l'hôpital.** [ʒə dwa mə ʀɑ̃dʀ a lɔpital]
Is there a doctor who speaks English?	**Y a-t-il un médecin qui parle anglais?** [jatil ɑ̃ medsɛ̃ ki paʀl ɑ̃glɛ]
It's an emergency.	**C'est urgent.** [sɛt yʀʒɑ̃]
I've been hurt.	**Je suis blessé(e).** [ʒə sɥi blɛse]
My leg is broken.	**Je me suis cassé une jambe.** [ʒə mə sɥi kase yn ʒɑ̃b]
I've lost a lot of blood.	**J'ai perdu beaucoup de sang.** [ʒe pɛʀdy bocu də sɑ̃]

AT THE PHARMACY

In France, pharmacies are generally small, but apart from dealing with prescriptions and selling various medications over the counter, they also have good perfume and cosmetics departments, and probably have someone on hand who can identify wild mushrooms, too. A *droguerie* is a different kind of establishment; it sells paints, cleaning products and other household goods.

I'm looking for a chemists.	**Je cherche une pharmacie.** [ʒə ʃɛrʃ yn farmasi]
Where's the duty pharmacy?	**Où se trouve la pharmacie de garde?** [u sə truv la farmasi də gard]
I have a prescription.	**J'ai une ordonnance.** [ʒe yn ɔrdɔnãs]
How do I take this medication?	**Comment faut-il prendre ce médicament?** [kɔmã fotil prãdr sə medikamã]
Swallow one tablet with water...	**Avalez un comprimé avec de l'eau...** [avale œ̃ kɔprime avɛk de lo]
... every three hours	**... toutes les trois heures** [tut le trwazœr]
... four times a day	**... quatre fois par jour** [katr fwa par jur]
... before/during/after meals	**... avant/avec/après les repas** [avã/avɛk/aprɛ le rəpa]
... in the morning/evening	**... le matin/le soir** [lə matɛ̃/lə swar]
... only if you're in pain	**... seulement en cas de douleur** [sœləmã ã ka də dulœr]
Could you recommend something for...	**Pouvez vous me conseiller quelque chose contre...?** [puve vu mə kɔ̃sɛje kɛlkə ʃoz kɔtr]

a hangover	**la gueule de bois** [la gœl də bwa]	hoarseness	**l'enrouement** [lãRuəmã]
acid stomach	**les brûlures d'estomac** [le bRylyR dεstoma]	insect bites	**les piqûres d'insectes** [le pikyR dɛ̃sɛkt]
		migraine	**la migraine** [la migRεn]
headaches	**les maux de tête** [le mo də tɛt]	trapped wind	**l'aérophagie** [laeRofaʒi]

Here is a list of items you can buy in a pharmacy, in case something's missing from your first-aid kit (*trousse de secours*).

I need a/an/some...   **Il me faut...**
                        [il mə fo]

analgesic	**un analgésique** [œ̃ nanalʒezik]	eye drops	**un collyre** [œ̃ kɔliR]
antibiotic	**un antibiotique** [œ̃ nãtibjotik]	granules	**des granulés** [de gRanyle]
antiseptic	**un antiseptique** [œ̃ nãtisεptik]	homeopathic remedy	**un remède homéopathique** [œ̃ Rəmεd ɔmeəpatik]
aspirin	**de l'aspirine** [də laspiRin]		
bandage	**un pansement** [œ̃ pãsmã]	ointment	**une pommade** [yn pɔmad]
capsules	**des gélules** [de ʒelyl]	pain-killer	**un calmant** [œ̃ kalmã]
condoms	**des préservatifs** [de pRezεRvatif]	penicillin	**de la pénicilline** [də la penisilin]
cotton wool	**du coton hydro-phile, de l'ouate** [dy kɔtɔ̃ idRɔfil] [də lwat]	pills	**des pilules** [de pilyl]
		sleeping pills	**des somnifères** [de sɔmnifɛR]
cough linctus	**du sirop pour la toux** [dy siRo puR la tu]	sticking plaster	**du sparadrap** [dy spaRadRa]
disinfectant	**du désinfectant** [dy dezɛ̃fɛktã]	sunblock	**de la crème solaire** [də la kRεm sɔlɛR]
ear plugs	**des boules Quiès** [de bul kjɛs]	vitamins	**des vitamines** [de vitamin]

95

AT THE DENTIST'S, AT THE OPTICIAN'S

All good travellers go to the dentist's before leaving home, but an accident can always happen…

I've broken a tooth.	**Je me suis cassé une dent.** [ʒə mə sɥi kase yn dɑ̃]
I've lost a filling.	**J'ai perdu un plombage.** [ʒe pɛʀdy œ̃ plɔ̃baʒ]
My crown has fallen out.	**Ma couronne est tombée.** [ma kuʀɔn ɛ tɔ̃be]
This tooth is aching.	**Cette dent me fait mal.** [sɛt dɑ̃ mə fɛ mal]
Can you give me a temporary treatment?	**Pouvez-vous me faire un traitement provisoire?** [puve vu mə fɛʀ œ̃ tʀɛtmɑ̃ pʀɔvizwaʀ]
Can you give me a local anaesthetic?	**Pouvez-vous me faire une anesthésie locale?** [puve vu mə fɛʀ yn anɛstezi lɔkal]

Drat it, you've lost a contact lens in the swimming pool? You need an optician (*un opticien*), quickly.

I've lost a contact lens.	**J'ai perdu un verre de contact.** [ʒe pɛʀdy œ̃ vɛʀ də kɔ̃takt]
Can you replace it?	**Pouvez-vous me le remplacer?** [puve vu mə lə ʀɑ̃plase]
Do you have disposable lenses?	**Avez-vous des verres de contact jetables?** [ave vu de vɛʀ də kɔ̃takt ʒətabl]
I've broken my glasses.	**J'ai cassé mes lunettes.** [ʒe kase me lynɛt]
Can you repair them?	**Pouvez-vous les réparer?** [puve vu le ʀepaʀe]

The Hard Facts

In this section we have included some general information together with phrases that will help you handle the practicalities of life in France, such as the telephone and money matters.

You will soon get the hang of the euro, even if the numerous tiny coins are a bit of a nuisance; as for weights and measures, the French use the metric system which is much easier than pounds and ounces. Metres and kilometres are used to measure distance; road speeds are indicated in kilometres per hour. Clothing sizes are in centimetres and grocery items are sold by grams and kilos. But half a kilo, 500 grams, is commonly called *une livre*, a pound, while 250 g is *une demi-livre*, half a pound. When buying food, it's handy to remember that 100 g is more or less equivalent to 4 ounces.

97

MONEY

You can draw money from cash distributors (*distributeurs automa-tiques*) at banks and post offices as long as you know your PIN number (NIP in French). You shouldn't have any problem using them as there's usually a language button to press at start-up, and you can do all transactions in English.

I need some money.	**J'ai besoin d'argent.** [ʒe bəzwɛ̃ daʀʒɑ̃]
I'm looking for a cash dispenser.	**Je cherche un distributeur automatique.** [ʒə ʃɛʀʃ œ̃ distʀibytœʀ ɔtɔmatik]
The machine has swallowed my card.	**Le distributeur a avalé ma carte.** [lə distʀibytœʀ a avale ma kaʀt]

If you want to change pounds sterling or dollars into euros, or to cash travellers cheques, go to a bank or a *bureau de change*. You will need to show proof of identity to cash your travellers cheques (and make sure you keep the numbers in a safe place). Large hotels can usually change money too; the exchange rate is posted up by reception. You can also withdraw cash in a bank with your credit card.

Where's the nearest bank?	**Où se trouve la banque la plus proche?** [u sə tʀuv la bɑ̃k la ply pʀɔʃ]
I'm looking for an exchange office.	**Je cherche un bureau de change.** [ʒə ʃɛʀʃ œ̃ byʀo də ʃɑ̃ʒ]
What's the exchange rate for pounds sterling/dollars?	**Quel est le taux de change de la livre sterling/du dollar?** [kɛl ɛ lə to də ʃɑ̃ʒ də la livʀ stɛʀliŋ/dy dɔlaʀ]
Do you charge a commission?	**Est-ce que vous prenez une commission?** [ɛskə vu pʀəne yn kɔmisjɔ̃]

I'd like to change £50.	**J'aimerais changer 50 livres.** [ʒɛmərɛ ʃɑ̃ʒe sɛ̃kɑ̃t livʀ]		

I'd like to change £50. | **J'aimerais changer 50 livres.**
[ʒɛmərɛ ʃɑ̃ʒe sɛ̃kɑ̃t livʀ]

I'd like to cash some travellers cheques. | **J'aimerais encaisser des chèques de voyage.**
[ʒɛmərɛ ɑ̃kɛse de ʃɛk də vwajaʒ]

I'd like to withdraw cash on my credit card. | **Je voudrais retirer de l'argent avec ma carte de crédit.**
[ʒə vudʀɛ ʀətiʀe də laʀʒɑ̃ avɛk ma kaʀt də kʀedi]

In small notes, please. | **En petites coupures, s'il vous plaît.**
[ɑ̃ pətit kupyʀ silvuplɛ]

Could you give me some small change? | **Pourriez-vous me faire de la monnaie?**
[puʀie vu mə fɛʀ də la mɔnɛ]

Where can I have money sent? | **Où puis-je me faire envoyer de l'argent?**
[u pɥiʒ mə fɛʀ ɑ̃vwajə də laʀʒɑ̃]

bank card	**une carte bancaire** [yn kaʀt bɑ̃kɛʀ]	guarantee card	**une carte d'identité bancaire** [yn kaʀt didɑ̃tite bɑ̃kɛʀ]
banknote	**un billet (de banque)** [œ̃ bije də bɑ̃k]	identity card	**une carte d'identité** [yn kaʀt didɑ̃tite]
cashier	**la caisse** [la kɛs]	money order	**un mandat** [œ̃ mɑ̃da]
coin	**une pièce** [yn pjɛs]	passport	**un passeport** [œ̃ paspɔʀ]
counter	**le guichet** [lə giʃe]	signature	**une signature** [yn siɲatyʀ]
currency	**des devises** [de dəviz]	VAT	**la TVA** [la tevea]
interest	**les intérêts** [lezɛ̃teʀɛ]		

COMMUNICATIONS

Time passes quickly when you're on holiday, but don't forget to keep in touch with your family and friends back home.

Telephone

It doesn't matter if you left your mobile (*un portable*) behind. French telephones work well and you can make an international call from any public phone. Some take coins but most work with a phonecard which you can buy in post offices and newspaper kiosks. Cafés also have public phones; they are usually downstairs, near the toilets. You have to dial all ten figures of the French phone numbers, which all begin with a zero.

I'd like a phone card.	**J'aimerais une carte de téléphone.** [ʒɛməʀɛ yn kaʀt də telefɔn]
Where's the nearest phone box?	**Où se trouve la cabine téléphonique la plus proche?** [u sə tʀuv la kabin telefɔnik la ply pʀɔʃ]
Can I use your phone?	**Puis-je me servir de votre téléphone?** [pɥiʒ mə sɛʀviʀ də vɔtʀ telefɔn]
It's for a local call.	**C'est pour un appel local.** [sɛ puʀ œ̃napɛl lɔkal]
Have you a phone directory?	**Avez-vous un annuaire téléphonique?** [ave vu œ̃nanɥɛʀ telefɔnik]
I'd like to reverse the charges.	**Je voudrais faire un appel en PCV.** [ʒə vudʀɛ fɛʀ œ̃napɛl ɑ̃ peseve]
Hello, can I speak to Jack?	**Allo, pourrais-je parler à Jack?** [alo puʀɛʒ paʀle a dʒak]
Please tell him that I called.	**Dites-lui que j'ai appelé, s'il vous plaît.** [dit lɥi kə ʒe apəle silvuplɛ]

Could you ask him to ring me back on number...?	**Pourriez-vous lui dire de me rappeler au numéro...?** [puʀie vu lui diʀ də mə ʀapəle o nymeʀo]
I didn't understand.	**Je n'ai pas compris.** [ʒə ne pa kɔ̃pʀi]
Could you say it again very slowly?	**Pourriez-vous le répéter très lentement?** [puʀie vu lə ʀepete tʀɛ lɑ̃təmɑ̃]
I can hardly hear you.	**Je vous entends très mal.** [ʒə vuzɑ̃tɑ̃ tʀɛ mal]

Post

When you buy your postcards, you can ask for the stamps at the same time. The postal service in France is called *La Poste*; mailboxes are yellow with the logo of a stylized blue bird.

I'm looking for a mailbox.	**Je cherche une boîte aux lettres.** [ʒə ʃɛʀʃ yn bwat o lɛtʀ]
Where is the post office?	**Où est le bureau de poste?** [u ɛ lə byʀo də pɔst]
I'd like to send this letter by airmail.	**J'aimerais envoyer cette lettre par avion.** [ʒɛməʀɛ ɑ̃vwaje sɛt lɛtʀ paʀ avjɔ̃]
first-class mail	**courrier prioritaire** [kuʀje pʀiɔʀitɛʀ]
second-class mail	**courrier économique** [kuʀje ekɔnɔmik]
recorded delivery	**recommandé** [ʀəkɔmɑ̃de]
I'd like stamps for Great Britain.	**J'aimerais des timbres pour la Grande-Bretagne.** [ʒɛməʀɛ de tɛ̃bʀ puʀ la gʀɑ̃d bʀətaɲ]

Where's the poste restante?	**Où se trouve la poste restante?** [u sə tʀuv la pɔst ʀɛstãt]
Have you any mail for me?	**Avez-vous du courrier pour moi?** [ave vu dy kuʀje puʀ mwa]
I'm expecting a parcel.	**J'attends un colis.** [ʒatã œ̃ kɔli]
Can I send a fax from here?	**Puis-je passer un fax depuis ici?** [pɥiʒ pase œ̃ faks dəpɥi isi]
How much is it per page?	**Quel est le tarif par page?** [kɛl ɛ lə taʀif paʀ paʒ]

Internet

Most big towns have a Cyber Café, generally somewhere near the main railway station, but with a bit of luck you may be able to surf the net (*surfer sur le net*) in your hotel.

I'm looking for an Internet café.	**Je cherche un cybercafé.** [ʒə ʃɛʀʃ œ̃ sibɛʀkafe]
Can I log onto the Internet here?	**Puis-je accéder au net depuis ici?** [pɥiʒ aksede o nɛt dəpɥi isi]
Is there a computer free?	**Y a-t-il un ordinateur de libre?** [jatil œ̃nɔʀdinatœʀ də libʀ]
Can I access with my computer?	**Puis-je me connecter avec mon ordinateur?** [pɥiʒ mə kɔnɛkte avɛk mɔ̃nɔʀdinatœʀ]
Can I print a document?	**Est-il possible d'imprimer un document?** [ɛtil pɔsibl dɛ̃pʀime œ̃ dɔkymã]
Do you provide webcams?	**Mettez-vous des webcams à disposition?** [mɛte vu de wɛbkam a dispozisjɔ̃]

How much does it cost per hour?	**Quel est le tarif horaire?** [kɛl ɛ lə taʀif ɔʀɛʀ]
The computer's crashed!	**L'ordinateur s'est planté!** [lɔʀdinatœʀ sɛ plãte]
What's your e-mail address?	**Quelle est ton adresse e-mail?** [kɛl ɛ tõnadʀɛs imel]
at	**arobase (@)** [aʀobaz]
dot	**point (.)** [pwɛ̃]
underline	**souligné (_)** [suliɲe]
hyphen	**trait d'union, tiret (-)** [tʀɛ dynjõ] [tiʀe]
capitals/lower case	**majuscules/minuscules** [maʒyskyl] [minyskyl]
Have you a web site ?	**As-tu un site web?** [aty œ̃ sit wɛb]
www	**www** [dublǝve dublǝve dublǝve]

PARLEZ-VOUS TEXTO?

If you start chatting to your new friends in French, or sending text messages (SMS or *textos*), you'll soon discover that you can be just as inventive in shorthand French as in English, perhaps even more so, as many syllables can be written in just one letter. M, for example, sounds just the same as *aime*, C as *c' est*, N as *haine*, K7 as *cassette*, and so on. Qu can be replaced by k: kwa instead of *quoi*, or by just q: qq1 instead of *quelqu' un*. A+ means *à plus (tard)*, i.e. See you later; and MDR (*mort de rire*) is the equivalent of LOL (laughing out loud).

WEATHER

If you're trying to break the ice, you could try talking about the weather!

What a lovely day!	**Quelle journée magnifique!** [kɛl ʒuʀne maɲifik]
The sun's shining.	**Le soleil brille.** [lə sɔlɛj bʀij]
The weather's fine.	**Il fait beau.** [il fɛ bo]
The temperature's going up/down.	**La température est en hausse/en baisse.** [la tɑ̃peʀatyʀ ɛt ɑ̃ os/ɑ̃ bɛs]
It's raining.	**Il pleut.** [il plø]
It's pouring down.	**Il pleut à verse/il pleut des cordes.** [il plø a vɛʀs] [il plø de kɔʀd]
What terrible weather!	**Quel temps pourri!** [kel tɑ̃ puʀi]
I'll have to buy an umbrella.	**Il faudra acheter un parapluie.** [il fodʀa aʃte œ̃ paʀaplɥi]
It's hard to get used to this climate.	**J'ai de la peine à m'habituer à ce climat!** [ʒe də la pɛn a mabitye a sə klima]
This is my favourite season.	**C'est la saison que je préfère.** [se la sɛzɔ̃ kə ʒə pʀefɛʀ]
What's the weather forecast for tomorrow?	**Quelles sont les prévisions météo pour demain?** [kɛl sɔ̃ le pʀevizjɔ̃ meteo puʀ dəmɛ̃]
Do you think it will be better than yesterday?	**Pensez-vous qu'il fera plus beau qu'hier?** [pɑ̃se vu kil fəʀa ply bo kjɛʀ]

spring	**printemps** [pʀɛ̃tɑ̃]	mild	**doux** [du]
breeze	**brise** [bʀiz]	rainbow	**arc-en-ciel** [aʀkɑ̃sjɛl]
clear	**dégagé** [degaʒe]	shower	**averse** [avɛʀs]
cool	**frais** [fʀɛ]	warm	**chaud** [ʃo]

summer	**été** [ete]	hot	**très chaud** [tʀɛ ʃo]
dry	**sec** [sɛk]	lightning	**éclairs** [eklɛʀ]
fine weather	**beau temps** [bo tɑ̃]	stifling	**étouffant** [etufɑ̃]
hail	**grêle** [gʀɛl]	storm	**tempête** [tɑ̃pɛt]
hailstones	**grêlons** [gʀɛlɔ̃]	sunny	**ensoleillé** [ɑ̃sɔlɛje]
heat	**chaleur** [ʃalœʀ]	thunder	**tonnerre** [tɔnɛʀ]
heat wave	**canicule** [kanikyl]	thunderstorm	**orage** [ɔʀaʒ]

autumn	**automne** [otɔn]	fog	**brouillard** [bʀujaʀ]
cloudy	**nuageux** [nɥaʒø]	overcast	**couvert** [kuvɛʀ]
cold	**froid** [fʀwa]	rain	**pluie** [plɥi]
damp	**humide** [ymid]	wet	**mouillé** [muje]

winter	**hiver** [ivɛʀ]	ice	**glace** [glas]
black ice	**verglas** [vɛʀgla]	snow(flake)	**(flocon de) neige** [flɔkɔ̃ də nɛʒ]
blizzard	**tempête de neige** [tɑ̃pɛt də nɛʒ]	snowfall	**chute de neige** [ʃyt də nɛʒ]
freezing	**glacial** [glasjal]	wind	**vent** [vɑ̃]

PUBLIC HOLIDAYS

Banks, post offices and most shops are closed on public holidays (*jours fériés*). Banks close early on the day preceding a public holiday. When the holiday falls on a Thursday or a Tuesday, people often take off the intervening Friday or Monday to make a four-day break, which they call *faire le pont*.

January 1	**le Jour de l'An** [lə juʀ də lɑ̃]	New Year's Day
March/April	**lundi de Pâques** [lœ̃di də pɑk]	Easter Monday
April/May	**l'Ascension** [lasɑ̃sjɔ̃]	Ascension Day
May 1	**la Fête du Travail** [la fɛt dy tʀavaj]	Labour Day
May 8	**l'Armistice** (1945) [laʀmistis]	VE Day
May/June	**lundi de Pentecôte** [lœ̃di də pɑ̃təkot]	Whit Monday
July 14	**la Fête nationale** [la fɛt nasjɔnal]	Bastille Day
August 15	**l'Assomption** [lasɔ̃psjɔ̃]	Assumption Day
November 1	**la Toussaint** [la tusɛ̃]	All Saints' Day
November 11	**l'Armistice** (1918) [laʀmistis]	Remembrance Day
December 25	**Noël** [nɔɛl]	Christmas Day

a day	**un jour** [œ̃ ʒuʀ]	evening	**le soir** [lə swaʀ]
morning	**le matin** [lə matɛ̃]	night	**la nuit** [la nɥi]
afternoon	**l'après-midi** [lapʀemidi]	today	**aujourd'hui** [oʒuʀdɥi]

a week	**une semaine** [yn səmɛn]	Thursday	**jeudi** [jødi]
Monday	**lundi** [lœ̃di]	Friday	**vendredi** [vɑ̃dRədi]
Tuesday	**mardi** [maRdi]	Saturday	**samedi** [samdi]
Wednesday	**mercredi** [mɛRkRədi]	Sunday	**dimanche** [dimɑ̃ʃ]

a year	**une année** [yn ane]	June	**juin** [ʒɥɛ̃]
a month	**un mois** [œ̃ mwa]	July	**juillet** [ʒɥije]
January	**janvier** [jɑ̃vje]	August	**août** [ut]
February	**février** [fevRje]	September	**septembre** [sɛptɑ̃bR]
March	**mars** [maRs]	October	**octobre** [ɔktɔbR]
April	**avril** [avRil]	November	**novembre** [nɔvɑ̃bR]
May	**mai** [mɛ]	December	**décembre** [desɑ̃bR]

three days ago	**il y a trois jours** [ilja tRwa juR]
last Monday	**lundi dernier** [lœ̃di dɛRnje]
last week	**la semaine passée** [la səmɛn pase]
next month	**le mois prochain** [lə mwa pRɔʃɛ̃]
in ten days	**dans dix jours** [dɑ̃ di juR]
a fortnight	**quinze jours, une quinzaine** [kɛ̃z juR] [yn kɛ̃zɛn]
a century	**un siècle** [œ̃ sjɛkl]

POLICE

If you have a serious problem, find a policeman (*un policier, un agent de police*) or go to the nearest police station. In France, the gendarmes belong to the army and patrol the motorways and main roads.

Remember to keep your valuables and papers in the hotel safe, lock your car and keep your personal belongings locked in the boot. In crowded places such as the metro, be wary of pickpockets.

Can you help me?	**Pouvez-vous m'aider?** [puve vu mɛde]
Where's the nearest police station?	**Où se trouve le poste de police le plus proche?** [u sə tʀuv lə pɔst də pɔlis lə ply pʀɔʃ]
I want to report a/an...	**Je veux signaler...** [ʒə vø siɲale]
... accident/mugging/theft	**... un accident/une agression/un vol** [œ̃naksidɑ̃] [yn agʀɛsjɔ̃] [œ̃ vɔl]
I'm being followed.	**Quelqu'un me suit.** [kɛlkœ̃ mə sɥi]
I've been attacked.	**On m'a attaqué(e).** [ɔ̃ ma atake]
My bag has been stolen.	**On a volé mon sac.** [ɔ̃na vɔle mɔ̃ sak]
I've lost my papers.	**J'ai perdu mes papiers.** [ʒe pɛʀdy me papje]
I have no money left.	**Je n'ai plus d'argent.** [ʒə ne ply daʀʒɑ̃]
My car's been broken into.	**On a forcé ma voiture.** [ɔ̃na fɔʀse ma vwatyʀ]
I need to contact my embassy/consulate.	**Je dois contacter mon ambassade/consulat.** [ʒə dwa kɔ̃sylte mɔ̃ ɑ̃basad/kɔ̃syla]

Dictionary

In the different chapters of this phrase book, we included alphabetical lists of vocabulary pertinent to the situation described: meeting people, accommodation, health, etc. Here you will find a dictionary of some 1000 words to help you increase your French vocabulary.

Most of the words listed here are not mentioned elsewhere in the book. We have tried to avoid giving terms whose meaning is obvious because of a similarity in the two languages, e.g. activity/*activité*. Even if you haven't the slightest notion of French you will find that many expressions seem familiar—after the Norman Conquest French was the official language in English court circles and much of this heritage is apparent in modern English.

In order to avoid confusion we have indicated the parts of speech and gender of French nouns (nm, nf, nm pl, nf pl).

A

able *adj*	**capable** *adj*
about *adv*	**environ** *adv*
accommodation *n*	**hébergement** *nm*
adaptor *n*	**adaptateur** *nm*
advertisement *n*	**publicité** *nf*
advice *n*	**conseil** *nm*
after *adv*	**après** *adv*
afternoon *n*	**après-midi** *nm*
against *prep*	**contre** *prép*
alarm clock *n*	**réveil** *nm*
all *pron*	**tout, toutes, tous** *pron*
allow *v*	**permettre** *v*
almost *adv*	**presque** *adv*
alone *adj*	**seul** *adj*
always *adv*	**toujours** *adv*
amazing *adj*	**étonnant** *adj*
amount *n*	**quantité** *nf*
ancestor *n*	**ancêtre** *nm*
and *conj*	**et** *conj*
anger *n*	**colère** *nf*
angry *adj*	**fâché** *adj*
ankle *n*	**cheville** *nf*
ant *n*	**fourmi** *nf*
appalled *adj*	**ulcéré** *adj*
appointment *n*	**rendez-vous** *nm*
arm *n*	**bras** *nm*
armchair *n*	**fauteuil** *nm*
arrow *n*	**flèche** *nf*
as well as *adv*	**outre** *prép*
ash tray *n*	**cendrier** *nm*
ask *v*	**demander** *v*
ATM *n*	**Bancomat** *nm*
available *adj*	**disponible** *adj*
awful *adj*	**affreux** *adj*

B

back *n*	**dos** *nm*
bag *n*	**sac** *nm*
balcony *n*	**balcon** *nm*
ball *n*	**balle** *nf* **ballon** *nm*
balloon *n*	**ballon** *nm*
barley *n*	**orge** *nf*
barn *n*	**grange** *nf*
bath *n*	**bain** *nm*
bathing costume *n*	**maillot de bain** *nm*
bathroom *n*	**salle de bains** *nf*
bathtub *n*	**baignoire** *nf*
battery *n*	**pile** *nf*
beach *n*	**plage** *nf*
bean (French) *n* (broad) *n*	**haricot** *nm* **fève** *nf*
bear *n*	**ours** *nm*
beard *n*	**barbe** *nf*
become *v*	**devenir** *v*
bed *n*	**lit** *nm*
bedroom *n*	**chambre à coucher** *nf*
bee *n*	**abeille** *nf*
before *adv*	**avant** *adv*
beg *v*	**mendier** *v*
beginner *n*	**débutant** *nm*
behind *adv*	**arrière** *adv* **derrière** *adv*
believe *v*	**croire** *v*
bell *n*	**cloche** *nf*
beneath *prep*	**dessous** *prép*
bicycle *n*	**vélo** *nm*
bill *n*	**addition** *nf*
binoculars *n pl*	**jumelles** *nf pl*
bird *n*	**oiseau** *nm*

birthday *n*	**anniversaire** *nm*	bucket *n*	**seau** *nm*
bitter *adj*	**amer** *adj*	building *n*	**bâtiment** *nm*
bladder *n*	**vessie** *nf*	bump *n*	**bosse** *nf*
blade *n*	**lame** *nf*	burial *n*	**enterrement** *nm*
bleed *v*	**saigner** *v*	burn *v*	**brûler** *v*
blind *adj*	**aveugle** *adj*	bush *n*	**buisson** *nm*
blister *n*	**ampoule** *nf*	business *n*	**affaires** *nf pl*
block *n*	**bloc** *nm*	but *conj*	**mais** *conj*
block *v*	**boucher** *v*	butterfly *n*	**papillon** *nm*
blood *n*	**sang** *nm*	buttock *n*	**fesse** *nf*
blouse *n*	**chemisier** *nm*	button *n*	**bouton** *nm*
blow *v*	**souffler** *v*	buy *v*	**acheter** *v*
boat *n*	**bateau** *nm*		
bolt *v*	**verrouiller** *v*		

C

bone *n*	**os** *nm*	calf *n*	**veau** *nm*
boned *adj*	**désossé** *adj*	call *v*	**appeler** *v*
book *n*	**livre** *nm*	camera *n*	**appareil photo** *nm*
book *v*	**réserver** *v*		
bookshop *n*	**librairie** *nf*	cancel *v*	**annuler** *v*
boring *adj*	**ennuyeux** *adj*	candle *n*	**bougie** *nf*
borrow *v*	**emprunter** *v*	cap *n*	**casquette** *nf*
bottle *n*	**bouteille** *nf*	car *n*	**voiture** *nf*
bottle (baby's) *n*	**biberon** *nm*	cardboard *n*	**carton** *nm*
boundary *n*	**enceinte** *nf*	carpet *n*	**tapis** *nm*
box *n*	**boîte** *nf*	carriage *n* (in a train)	**wagon** *nm*
bra *n*	**soutien-gorge** *nm*		
bread *n*	**pain** *nm*	cartoon *n*	**dessin animé** *nm*
break *v*	**casser** *v*	cash desk *n*	**caisse** *nf*
breakfast *n*	**petit-déjeuner** *nm*	cash machine *n*	**distributeur automatique** *nm*
breast *n*	**sein** *nm*	cat *n*	**chat** *nm*
breathe *v*	**respirer** *v*	ceiling *n*	**plafond** *nm*
brick *n*	**brique** *nf*	chair *n*	**chaise** *nf*
bring *v*	**amener** *v*	chance *n*	**hasard** *nm*
brown *adj*	**brun** *adj*	change *n*	**monnaie** *nf*
bruise *n*	**bleu** *nm*	chat *v*	**bavarder** *v*
brush *n*	**brosse** *nf*	cheap *adj*	**bon marché** *adj*

cheek n	**joue** nf	corridor n	**couloir** nm
cheeky n	**impertinent** adj	cost v	**coûter** v
cheese n	**fromage** nm	cotton wool n	**ouate** nf
chess n	**échecs** nm pl	cough v	**tousser** v
chest n	**poitrine** nf	courtyard n	**cour** nf
chicken n	**poulet** nm	cow n	**vache** nf
chickenpox n	**varicelle** nf	crazy adj	**fou** adj
child n	**enfant** nm	cream n	**crème** nf
chin n	**menton** nm	creature n	**bête** nf
chips n pl	**frites** nf pl	crockery n	**vaisselle** nf
choose v	**choisir** v	crumb n	**miette** nf
chopper n	**hachoir** nm	cry v	**pleurer** v
clean adj	**propre** adj	cupboard n	**placard** nm
clean v	**nettoyer** v	currency n	**devises** nf pl
clearing n	**clairière** nf	curtain n	**rideau** nm
clever adj	**intelligent** adj	curve n	**courbe** nf
cliff n	**falaise** nf	cushion n	**coussin** nm
cloakroom n	**vestiaire** nm	customs n pl	**douane** nf
clock n	**horloge** nf	(traditions) n pl	**coutumes** nf pl
close v	**fermer** v	cut v	**couper** v
clothing n	**habits** nm pl		
cloud n	**nuage** nm		
coal n	**charbon** nm	**D**	
coat n	**manteau** nm		
cock n	**coq** nm	daily adj	**quotidien** adj
cockroach n	**cafard** nm	damage v	**abîmer** v
cold adj	**froid** adj	damage n	**dégâts** nm pl
come v	**venir** v	damp adj	**humide** adj
common adj	**commun** adj	dangerous adj	**dangereux** adj
compass n	**boussole** nf	dare v	**oser** v
(geometry)	**compas** nm	day n	**jour** nm
compulsory adj	**obligatoire** adj	dazed adj	**hébété** adj
computer n	**ordinateur** nm	deaf adj	**sourd** adj
condom n	**préservatif** nm	decorate v	**décorer** v
congratulations!	**félicitations!**	defeat v	**vaincre** v
n pl	nf pl	delay n	**retard** nm
core n	**noyau** nm	delicatessen n	**traiteur** nm
corkscrew n	**tire-bouchon** nm	dental floss n	**fil dentaire** nm
		deny v	**nier** v

deposit (hotel) *n*	**arrhes** *nf pl*
(refundable)	**caution** *nf*
diary *n*	**journal intime** *nm*
dice *n*	**dé** *nm*
diet *n*	**régime** *nm*
difficult *adj*	**difficile** *adj*
dimple *n*	**fossette** *nf*
dining room *n*	**salle à manger** *nf*
dirty *adj*	**sale** *adj*
disappear *v*	**disparaître** *v*
disappointed *adj*	**déçu** *adj*
disaster *n*	**désastre** *nm*
discover *v*	**découvrir** *v*
disgust *n*	**dégoût** *nm*
disgusting *adj*	**infect** *adj*
disposable nappies *n pl*	**couches-culottes** *nf pl*
district *n*	**quartier** *nm*
disturb *v*	**déranger** *v*
dizzying *adj*	**vertigineux** *adj*
do *v*	**faire** *v*
dog *n*	**chien** *nm*
doll *n*	**poupée** *nf*
dolphin *n*	**dauphin** *nm*
door *n*	**porte** *nf*
doorbell *n*	**sonnette** *nf*
draught *n*	**courant d'air** *nm*
draughts *n pl*	**jeu de dames** *nm*
drawing *n*	**dessin** *nm*
dress *n*	**robe** *nf*
dressed *adj*	**habillé** *adj*
drink *v*	**boire** *v*
drink *n*	**boisson** *nf*
drive *v*	**conduire** *v*
driver *n*	**conducteur** *nm*
drop *v*	**laisser tomber** *v*

drop *n*	**goutte** *nf*
drown *v*	**noyer** *v*
drunk *adj*	**ivre** *adj*
dry *v*	**sécher** *v*
duck *n*	**canard** *nm*
dull *adj*	**terne** *adj*

E

ear *n*	**oreille** *nf*
early *adv*	**tôt** *adv*
earn *v*	**gagner** *v*
earth *n*	**terre** *nf*
east *n*	**est** *nm*
eat *v*	**manger** *v*
egg *n*	**œuf** *nm*
embrace *v*	**étreindre** *v*
emergency *n*	**urgence** *nf*
empty *adj*	**vide** *adj*
end *n*	**fin** *nf*
engaged *adj* (toilets)	**occupé** *adj*
enjoy *v* (oneself)	**apprécier** *v* **s'amuser** *v*
enough *adv*	**assez** *adv*
everyone *pron*	**tout le monde** *loc pron*
except *prep*	**sauf** *prép*
exhausted *adj*	**épuisé** *adj*
exhibition *n*	**exposition** *nf*
expensive *adj*	**cher** *adj*
extra *adj*	**supplémentaire** *adj*
eye *n*	**œil** *nm*
eyebrow *n*	**sourcil** *nm*
eyelash *n*	**cil** *nm*
eyelid *n*	**paupière** *nf*
eyesight *n*	**vue** *nf*

F

face *n*	**visage** *nm*
face *v*	**faire face à** *v*
factory *n*	**usine** *nf*
failure *n*	**échec** *nm*
faith *n*	**foi** *nf*
fame *n*	**gloire** *nf*
family *n*	**famille** *nf*
far *adv*	**loin** *adv*
farm *n*	**ferme** *nf*
farmyard *n*	**basse-cour** *nf*
fasten *v*	**attacher** *v*
fat *adj*	**gros** *adj*
fear *n*	**peur** *nf*
feather *n*	**plume** *nf*
feeling *n*	**sentiment** *nm*
fees *n pl*	**honoraires** *nm pl*
field *n*	**champ** *nm*
fight *n*	**bagarre** *nf*
final *adj*	**ultime** *adj*
find *v*	**trouver** *v*
fine *n*	**amende** *nf*
fine *adj*	**fin** *adj*, **bien** *adv*
finger *n*	**doigt** *nm*
fire *n*	**feu** *nm* **incendie** *nm*
fireplace *n*	**cheminée** *nf*
first *adj*	**premier** *adj*
fishhook *n*	**hameçon** *nm*
flag *n*	**drapeau** *nm*
flesh *n*	**chair** *nf*
flight *n*	**vol** *nm*
flirt *v*	**flirter** *v*
floor *n*	**plancher** *nm*
flower *n*	**fleur** *nf*
flu *n*	**grippe** *nf*
fly *n*	**mouche** *nf*

fly *v*	**voler** *v*
follow *v*	**suivre** *v*
food *n*	**nourriture** *nf*
foot *n*	**pied** *nm*
football ground *n*	**terrain de foot** *nm*
forehead *n*	**front** *nm*
foreigner *n*	**étranger** *nm*
forest *n*	**forêt** *nf*
forget *v*	**oublier** *v*
fortnight *n*	**quinzaine** *nf*
fountain *n*	**jet d'eau** *nm*
four-wheel-drive vehicle *n*	**4x4** *nm* **(quatre-quatre)**
fox *n*	**renard** *nm*
fraud *n*	**supercherie** *nf*
freckle *n*	**tache de rousseur** *nf*
free *adj*	**gratuit** *adj* **libre** *adj*
freedom *n*	**liberté** *nf*
freeze *v*	**geler** *v* **congeler** *v*
friend *n*	**ami** *nm*
friendship *n*	**amitié** *nf*
frying pan *n*	**poêle** *nf*
full *adj*	**plein** *adj*
funny *adj*	**drôle** *adj*

G

game *n*	**jeu** *nm*
garden *n*	**jardin** *nm*
gauge *n*	**jauge** *nf*
gem *n*	**bijou** *nm*
generous *adj*	**généreux** *adj*
genuine *adj*	**véritable** *adj*
ghost *n*	**fantôme** *nm*

gift *n*	**cadeau** *nm*
give *v*	**donner** *v*
give back *v*	**rendre** *v*
glass *n*	**verre** *nm*
glove *n*	**gant** *nm*
glue *n*	**colle** *nf*
go *v*	**aller** *v*
go back *v*	**retourner** *v*
goal *n*	**but** *nm*
goat *n*	**chèvre** *nf*
gold *n*	**or** *nm*
goldsmith *n*	**orfèvre** *nm*
grass *n*	**herbe** *nf*
graze *n*	**écorchure** *nf*
graze (animal) *v* (scratch)	**paître** *v* **écorcher** *v*
greet *v*	**saluer** *v*
greetings *n pl*	**salutations** *nf pl*
grocery *n*	**épicerie** *nf*
ground floor *n*	**rez-de-chaussée** *nm*

H

habit *n*	**habitude** *nf*
hair (on head) *n* (on body)	**cheveux** *nm pl* **poil** *nm*
hairdresser *n*	**coiffeur** *nm*
half-board *n*	**demi-pension** *nf*
ham *n*	**jambon** *nm*
hand *n*	**main** *nf*
handbag *n*	**sac à main** *nm*
handicrafts *n pl*	**artisanat** *nm*
handkerchief *n*	**mouchoir** *nm*
handlebars *n pl*	**guidon** *nm*
hangover *n*	**gueule de bois** *nf*
harass *v*	**harceler** *v*
hard *adj*	**dur** *adj*

hard-boiled egg *n*	**œuf dur** *nm*
hardware shop *n*	**quincaillerie** *nf*
harm *v*	**nuire** *v*
harvest *n* (grapes)	**récolte** *nf* **vendanges** *nf pl*
haste *n*	**hâte** *nf*
hat *n*	**chapeau** *nm*
hate *v*	**détester** *v*
hatred *n*	**haine** *nf*
haughty *adj*	**hautain** *adj*
have *v*	**avoir** *v*
hayfever *n*	**rhume des foins** *nm*
hazelnut *n*	**noisette** *nf*
head *n*	**tête** *nf*
hear *v*	**entendre** *v*
heart *n*	**cœur** *nm*
heavy *adj*	**lourd** *adj*
hell *n*	**enfer** *nm*
help *n*	**aide** *nf*
hem *n*	**ourlet** *nm*
hen *n*	**poule** *nf*
here *adv*	**ici** *adv*
hiccoughs *n*	**hoquet** *nm*
hiking *n*	**randonnée** *nf*
hill *n*	**colline** *nf*
hip *n*	**hanche** *nf*
hire *v*	**louer** *v*
hit *v*	**frapper** *v*
hitchhiking *n*	**autostop** *nm*
hole *n*	**trou** *nm*
holidays *n pl*	**vacances** *nf pl*
home *n*	**maison** *nf*
honeymoon *n*	**lune de miel** *nf*
hope *n*	**espoir** *nm*
horn (car) *n* (instrument)	**klaxon** *nm* **cor** *nm*

115

hornet *n*	**frelon** *nm*
horror *n*	**horreur** *nf*
horse *n*	**cheval** *nm*
hot *adj*	**chaud** *adj*
house *n*	**maison** *nf*
hug *v*	**serrer dans ses bras** *v*
hunger *n*	**faim** *nf*
hurricane *n*	**ouragan** *nm*

I

ice *n*	**glace** *nf*
ice cream *n*	**crème glacée** *nf*
ice cube *n*	**glaçon** *nm*
icebox *n*	**glacière** *nf*
idea *n*	**idée** *nf*
identity *n*	**identité** *nf*
ill *adj*	**malade** *adj*
illuminate *v*	**illuminer** *v*
illustrate *v*	**illustrer** *v*
immortal *adj*	**immortel** *adj*
implement *n*	**ustensile** *nm*
included *adj*	**compris** *adj*
income *n*	**revenu** *nm*
infinite *adj*	**infini** *adj*
inhabitant *n*	**habitant** *nm*
injection *n*	**piqûre** *nf*
injured *adj*	**blessé** *adj*
injury	**blessure** *nf*
ink *n*	**encre** *nf*
insect *n*	**insecte** *nm*
insect bite *n*	**piqûre d'insecte** *nf*
insulating *adj*	**isolant** *adj*
insurance *n*	**assurance** *nf*
interesting *adj*	**intéressant** *adj*
intimate *adj*	**intime** *adj*

invoice *n*	**facture** *nf*
ironing *n*	**repassage** *nm*
island *n*	**île** *nf*
isolated *adj*	**isolé** *adj*
itch *v*	**démanger** *v*
ivy *n*	**lierre** *nm*

J

jacket *n*	**veste** *nf*
jam *n*	**confiture** *nf*
jar *n*	**bocal** *nm*
jealous *adj*	**jaloux** *adj*
jelly *n*	**gelée** *nf*
jewel *n*	**joyau** *nm*
job *n*	**travail** *nm* **profession** *nf*
join *v*	**joindre** *v*
joke *n*	**blague** *nf*
juice *n*	**jus** *nm*
juicy *adj*	**juteux** *adj*

K

keep *v*	**garder** *v*
kennel *n*	**niche** *nf*
kernel *n*	**noyau** *nm*
key *n*	**clé** *nf*
kidney *n*	**rein** *nm*
kind *adj*	**aimable** *adj*
kind *n*	**sorte** *nf*
king *n*	**roi** *nm*
kiss *n*	**baiser** *nm*
kiss *v*	**embrasser** *v*
kitchen *n*	**cuisine** *nf*
knee *n*	**genou** *nm*
kneel down *v*	**s'agenouiller** *v*

knife *n*	**couteau** *nm*	lemon *n*	**citron** *nm*
knot *n*	**nœud** *nm*	length *n*	**longueur** *nf*
knot *v*	**nouer** *v*	lens *n*	**lentille** *nf*
know (person) *v*	**connaître** *v*	lentils *n pl*	**lentilles** *nf pl*
(thing)	**savoir** *v*	level *n*	**niveau** *nm*
		library *n*	**bibliothèque** *nf*
		lifeguard *n*	**maître-nageur** *nm*

L

label *n*	**étiquette** *nf*	lift *n*	**ascenseur** *nm*
lace *n*	**dentelle** *nf*	lift *v*	**élever** *v*
(shoe)	**lacet** *nm*	light *n*	**lumière** *nf*
lacquer *n*	**laque** *nf*	light *adj*	**léger** *adj*
ladder *n*	**échelle** *nf*	lightbulb *n*	**ampoule** *nf*
lake *n*	**lac** *nm*	lighter *n*	**briquet** *nm*
lamp *n*	**lampe** *nf*	lime (tree) *n*	**tilleul** *nm*
land *v*	**atterrir** *v*	(fruit)	**citron vert** *nm*
land *n*	**terrain** *nm*	lip *n*	**lèvre** *nf*
landing *n*	**atterrissage** *nm*	liquid *n*	**liquide** *nm*
landscape *n*	**paysage** *nm*	listen *v*	**écouter** *v*
last *adj*	**dernier** *adj*	little *adj*	**petit** *adj*
late *adv*	**tard** *adv*	a little *adv*	**peu** *adv*
laugh *v, n*	**rire** *v, nm*	live *v*	**vivre** *v*
law *n*	**loi** *nf*, **droit** *nm*	live in *v*	**habiter** *v*
lawn *n*	**gazon** *nm*	liver *n*	**foie** *nm*
lazy *adj*	**paresseux** *adj*	living room *n*	**salon** *nm*
lead *n*	**plomb** *nm*	location *n*	**emplacement** *nm*
lead *v*	**mener** *v*		
	conduire *v*	lock *v*	**fermer à clé** *v*
leaf *n*	**feuille** *nf*	lodgings *n pl*	**logement** *nm*
learn *v*	**apprendre** *v*	lonely *adj*	**seul** *adj*
leave *v*	**laisser** *v*, **partir** *v*	long-sighted *adj*	**presbyte** *adj*
left *adj*	**gauche** *adj*	look at *v*	**regarder** *v*
left-handed *adj*	**gaucher** *adj*	look for *v*	**chercher** *v*
left-luggage office *n*	**consigne** *nf*	loose *v*	**perdre** *v*
		lorry *n*	**camion** *nm*
leg *n*	**jambe** *nf*	louse *n*	**pou** *nm*
leisure activities *n pl*	**loisirs** *nm pl*	love *v*	**aimer** *v*
		lower *v*	**baisser** *v*

117

luck n	**chance** nf	moor v	**amarrer** v
luggage n	**bagages** nm pl	moor n	**lande** nf
lukewarm adj	**tiède** adj	mosquito n	**moustique** nm
lunch n	**déjeuner** nm	motorway n	**autoroute** nf
lung n	**poumon** nm	mouldy adj	**moisi** adj
		mountain n	**montagne** nf
		mountain bike n	**vélo tout-terrain** nm

M

mad adj	**fou** adj	mouse n	**souris** nf
magnifying glass n	**loupe** nf	mouth n	**bouche** nf
		mugging n	**agression** nf
mail n	**courrier** nm	mumps n pl	**oreillons** nm pl
make v	**faire** v	mussel n	**moule** nf
manager n	**gérant** nm		
map (country) n	**carte** nf		

N

(city)	**plan** nm	nail (tool) n	**clou** nm
market n	**marché** nm	(finger, toe)	**ongle** nm
marry v	**épouser** v	nail varnish n	**vernis à ongles** nm
masterpiece n	**chef-d'œuvre** nm		
matches n pl	**allumettes** nf pl	naked adj	**nu** adj
meadow n	**pré** nm	narrow adj	**étroit** adj
meal n	**repas** nm	native adj	**natif** adj
meat n	**viande** nf	navel n	**nombril** nm
melt v	**fondre** v	near adv	**près** adv
mileage n	**kilométrage** nm	neat adj	**net** adj
milk n	**lait** nm	(without ice)	**sans glaçons** loc
mince v	**émincer** v	neck n	**cou** nm
mirror n	**miroir** nm	need n	**besoin** nm
misfortune n	**infortune** nf	neglect v	**négliger** v
miss v	**manquer** v	nerve n	**nerf** nm
misunderstanding n	**malentendu** nm	nervous adj	**nerveux** adj
		nest n	**nid** nm
mobile phone n	**téléphone mobile** nm	neutral adj	**neutre** adj
		never adv	**jamais** adv
money n	**argent** nm	new adj	**neuf** adj
monk n	**moine** nm		**nouveau** adj
monkey n	**singe** nm		
moon n	**lune** nf	news n pl	**nouvelles** nf pl

newspaper *n*	**journal** *nm*
next *adj*	**prochain** *adj*
nibble *v*	**grignoter** *v*
nice *adj*	**gentil** *adj*
night *n*	**nuit** *nf*
noise *n*	**bruit** *nm*
noodles *n pl*	**nouilles** *nf pl*
nose *n*	**nez** *nm*
nostril *n*	**narine** *nf*
nothing *pron*	**rien** *pron ind*
novel *n*	**roman** *nm*
now *adv*	**maintenant** *adv*
noxious *adj*	**nocif** *adj*
nude *n*	**nu** *nm*
number *n*	**nombre** *nm*
(figure)	**numéro** *nm*
numerous *adj*	**nombreux** *adj*
nun *n*	**nonne** *nf*
nurse *n*	**infirmière** *nf*
nutcracker *n*	**casse-noix** *nm*

O

oats *n pl*	**avoine** *nf*
obey *v*	**obéir** *v*
often *adv*	**souvent** *adv*
oil *n*	**huile** *nf*
old *adj*	**vieux** *adj*
only *adv*	**seulement** *adv*
open *v*	**ouvrir** *v*
opinion *n*	**avis** *nm*
opposite *n*	**contraire** *nm*
order *v*	**commander** *v*
ornament *n*	**bibelot** *nm*
other *pron, adj*	**autre** *pron, adj*
outraged *adj*	**outré** *adj*
owe *v*	**devoir** *v*
owl *n*	**hibou** *nm*

P

padlock *n*	**cadenas** *nm*
pain *n*	**douleur** *nf*
pain-killer *n*	**analgésique** nm
palm (hand) *n*	**paume** *nf*
(tree)	**palmier** *nm*
paper *n*	**papier** *nm*
parade *n*	**défilé** *nm*
parcel *n*	**colis** *nm*
pasta *n*	**pâtes** *nf pl*
path *n*	**chemin** *nm*
pavement *n*	**trottoir** *nm*
pay *v*	**payer** *v*
peace *n*	**paix** *nf*
peanut *n*	**cacahuète** *nf*
pebble *n*	**caillou**
(on the beach)	**galet** *nm*
pedestrian *n*	**piéton** *nm*
pen *n*	**stylo** *nm*
pencil *n*	**crayon** *nm*
performance *n*	**séance** *nf*
perhaps *adv*	**peut-être** *adv*
petrol *n*	**essence** *nf*
pewter *n*	**étain** *nm*
phone directory *n*	**annuaire téléphonique** *nm*
physiotherapist *n*	**kinésithérapeute** *nm*
picture *n*	**tableau** *nm*
piece *n*	**morceau** *nm*
pig *n*	**cochon** *nm*
pin *n*	**épingle** *nf*
pipe (smoke) *n*	**pipe** *nf*
(water, oil etc.)	**tuyau** *nm*
plane *n*	**avion** *nm*
plant *n*	**plante** *nf*
platform (rail) *n*	**quai** *nm*

119

play *v*	**jouer** *v*		record *n*	**disque** *nm*
pleasant *adj*	**agréable** *adj*		record *v*	**enregistrer** *v*
pond *n*	**étang** *nm*		reduction *n*	**rabais** *nm*
poor *adj*	**pauvre** *adj*		refund *n*	**remboursement** *nm*
postman *n*	**facteur** *nm*			
potato crisps *n pl*	**chips** *nf pl*		relax *v*	**décompresser** *v*
			remember *v*	**se souvenir** *v*
pound *n*	**livre** *nf*		rent *n*	**loyer** *nm*
power *n*	**pouvoir** *nm*		repair *v*	**réparer** *v*
pregnant *adj*	**enceinte** *adj*		rest *n*	**repos** *nm*
pretty *adj*	**joli** *adj*		return *v*	**retourner** *v*
pride *n*	**orgueil** *nm*		rice *n*	**riz** *nm*
primus stove *n*	**réchaud** *nm*		rich *adj*	**riche** *adj*
printer *n*	**imprimante** *nf*		right (to be) *v*	**avoir raison** *v*
	imprimeur *nm*		right *adj*	**juste** *adj*
			right-handed *adj*	**droitier** *adj*
			rim *n*	**bord** *nm*

Q

quarrel *n*	**querelle** *nf*		ring *n*	**bague** *nf*
quay *n*	**quai** *nm* (d'un port)		ring *v*	**sonner** *v*
			ripe *adj*	**mûr** *adj*
queen *n*	**reine** *nf*		rise *n*	**hausse** *nf*
quiet *adj*	**calme** *adj*		rise *v*	**s'élever** *v*
quit *v*	**quitter** *v*		river *n* (tributary)	**fleuve** *nm* **rivière** *nf*
			rock *n*	**rocher** *nm*

R

			rock *v*	**se balancer** *v*
			roll *v*	**rouler** *v*
rabbit *n*	**lapin** *nm*		roof *n*	**toit** *nm*
raid *v*	**dévaliser** *v*		round *adj*	**rond** *adj*
raincoat *n*	**imperméable** *nm*		route *n*	**itinéraire** *nm*
rape *n*	**viol** *nm*		row *v*	**ramer** *v*
rate *n*	**tarif** *nm*		rubbish *n*	**ordures** *nf pl*
read *v*	**lire** *v*		rucksack *n*	**sac à dos** *nm*
reason *n*	**raison** *nf*		rude *adj*	**grossier** *adj*
receipt *n*	**reçu** *nm*		rummage *v*	**fouiller** *v*
receive *v*	**recevoir** *v*		run *v* (liquid)	**courir** *v* **couler** *v*
recognise *v*	**reconnaître** *v*			
recommend *v*	**conseiller** *v*		run-down *adj*	**délabré** *adj*

S

safe *n*	**coffre-fort** *nm*
safety pin *n*	**épingle de nourrice** *nf*
sand *n*	**sable** *nm*
say *v*	**dire** *v*
scarf *n*	**écharpe** *nf*
school *n*	**école** *nf*
scissors *n pl*	**ciseaux** *nm pl*
scratch *n*	**égratignure** *nf*
scratch *v*	**gratter** *v*
screwdriver *n*	**tourne-vis** *nm*
sea *n*	**mer** *nf*
seagull *n*	**mouette** *nf*
seat *n*	**siège** *nm*
see *v*	**voir** *v*
seed *n*	**graine** *nf*
sell *v*	**vendre** *v*
send *v*	**envoyer** *v*
sense *n*	**sens** *nm*
serial *n*	**feuilleton** *nm*
serious *adj*	**grave** *adj*
sewer *n*	**égoût** *nm*
shadow *n*	**ombre** *nf*
shade *n*	**ombre** *nf*
shake (before opening) *v*	**agiter** *v* (avant d'ouvrir)
shame *n*	**honte** *nf*
share *v*	**partager** *v*
sheep *n inv*	**mouton** *nm*
sheet *n*	**drap** *nm*
shelter *n*	**abri** *nm*
shin *n*	**mollet** *nm*
shipwreck *n*	**naufrage** *nm*
shirt *n*	**chemise** *nf*
shock absorbers *n pl*	**amortisseurs** *nm pl*
shoe *n*	**chaussure** *nf*
shoelace *n*	**lacet** *nm*
shop *n*	**magasin** *nm*
shopping *n*	**achats** *nm pl*
shorten *v*	**raccourcir** *v*
short-sighted *adj*	**myope** *adj*
shoulder *n*	**épaule** *nf*
shout *v*	**crier** *v*
show *n*	**spectacle** *nm*
show *v*	**indiquer** *v* **montrer** *v*
showcase *n*	**vitrine** *nf*
shower *n*	**douche** *nf* **ondée** *nf*
shrub *n*	**arbuste** *nm*
shutter *n*	**volet** *nm*
shy *adj*	**timide** *adj*
sign on *v*	**s'inscrire** *v*
silly *adj*	**bête** *adj*
silver *adj*	**argent** *adj*
since *prép, adv*	**depuis** *prép, adv*
sing *v*	**chanter** *v*
sit down *v*	**s'asseoir** *v*
size *n*	**taille** *nf*
sketch *v*	**esquisser** *v*
skin *n*	**peau** *nf*
skirt *n*	**jupe** *nf*
skittles *n pl*	**quilles** *nf pl*
skull *n*	**crâne** *nm*
sleep *v*	**dormir** *v*
slow *adj*	**lent** *adj*
smell *n*	**odeur** *nf*
smell *v*	**sentir** *v*
smile *v, n*	**sourire** *v, nm*
smoke *n*	**fumée** *nf*
smooth *adj*	**lisse** *adj*
snail *n*	**escargot** *nm*
snake *n*	**serpent** *nm*

121

sneeze v	**éternuer** v	stomach n	**estomac** nm
snore v	**ronfler** v	stone n	**pierre** nf
snow n	**neige** nf	stop v	**arrêter** v
soap n	**savon** nm	story n	**histoire** nf
sock n	**chaussette** nf	straight adj	**droit** adj
soft adj	**mou** adj	strange adj	**étrange** adj
software n	**logiciel** nm	street n	**rue** nf
sole n	**semelle** nf	strength n	**force** nf
something pron	**quelque chose** loc ind	string n	**ficelle** nf
		stripe n	**rayure** nf
sometimes adv	**quelquefois** adv	stroll v	**déambuler** v
song n	**chanson** nf	strong adj	**fort** adj
soon adv	**bientôt** adv	student n	**étudiant** nm
sparrow n	**moineau** nm	suitcase n	**valise** nf
speak v	**parler** v	sulky adj	**boudeur** adj
spelling n	**orthographe** nf	sun n	**soleil** nm
spend v	**dépenser** v	sunbathe v	**bronzer** v
spider n	**araignée** nf	sunstroke n	**insolation** nf
spine n	**colonne vertébrale** nf	survive v	**survivre** v
		swallow v	**avaler** v
spoil v	**gâter** v	swallow n	**hirondelle** nf
spoon n	**cuiller** nf	sweet n	**bonbon** nm
spot n	**bouton** nm **endroit** nm	sweet adj	**doux** adj (sucré)
		swim v	**nager** v
sprain n	**entorse** nf	swimming pool n	**piscine** nf
square adj	**carré** adj	switch n	**interrupteur** nm
stable n	**étable** nf	switch v	**échanger** v
staircase n	**escalier** nm		
stamp n	**timbre** nm		
standing adj	**debout** adv	**_T_**	
star n	**étoile** nf	tablecloth n	**nappe** nf
start v	**commencer** v	tail n	**queue** nf
station n	**gare** nf	take v	**emmener** v
stay v	**rester** v	take away v (food)	**emporter** v
stay n	**séjour** nm		
steal v	**voler** v (dérober)	take off n	**décollage** nm
steel n	**acier** nm	take off v	**ôter** v
stiff adj	**raide** adj	talk v	**parler** v

taste v	**goûter** v	tooth n	**dent** nf
tastebuds n pl	**papilles** nf pl	toothbrush n	**brosse à dents** nf
tax n	**impôt** nm	toothpaste n	**dentifrice** nm
tea n	**thé** nm	top n	**haut** nm
team n	**équipe** nf	(toy)	**toupie** nf
tear v	**déchirer** v	tortoise n	**tortue** nf
tear v	**larme** nf	touch v	**toucher** v
tease v	**taquiner** v	town n	**ville** nf
teddy bear n	**nounours** nm	toy n	**jouet** nm
tell v	**raconter** v	track n	**piste** nf
theft n	**vol** nm	traffic jam n	**embouteillage** nm
there adv	**là** adv		
thief n	**voleur** nm	tramp n	**clochard** nm
thigh n	**cuisse** nf	translate v	**traduire** v
thimble n	**dé à coudre** nm	travel v	**voyager** v
thing n	**chose** nf	tray n	**plateau** nm
thirst n	**soif** nf	tree n	**arbre** nm
threshold n	**seuil** nm	tribute n	**hommage** nm
throat n	**gorge** nf	truth n	**vérité** nf
throw v	**jeter** v	try v	**essayer** v
thumb n	**pouce** nm	tube n	**tuyau** nm
ticket office n	**guichet** nm	turn off v	**éteindre** v
tide n	**marée** nf	turnstile n	**tourniquet** nm
tidy up v	**ranger** v	twist v	**tordre** v
tie v	**attacher** v		
tile n	**tuile** nf		
timely adj	**opportun** adj	**U**	
timetable n	**horaire** nm		
tin n	**boîte** nf	ugly adj	**laid** adj
tin-opener n	**ouvre-boîte** nm	umbrella n	**parapluie** nm
tip n	**pourboire** nm	unbelievable adj	**incroyable** adj
tired adj	**fatigué** adj	understand v	**comprendre** v
toad n	**crapaud** nm	unit n	**unité** nf
today adv	**aujourd'hui** adv	unite v	**unir** v
toe n	**doigt de pied** nm	until prep	**jusqu'à** prép
tongue n	**langue** nf	use v	**utiliser** v
tonsils n pl	**amygdales** nf pl	useful adj	**utile** adj
tool n	**outil** nm	usherette n	**ouvreuse** nf
		usually adv	**d'habitude** loc

V

veal *n*	**veau** *nm*
vegetable *n*	**légume** *nm*
vein *n*	**veine** *nf*
vest *n*	**maillot de corps** *nm*
vineyard *n*	**vignoble** *nm*
voice *n*	**voix** *nf*

W

wait *v*	**attendre** *v*
wake up *v*	**réveiller** *v*
wall *n*	**mur** *nm*
wallet *n*	**portefeuille** *nm*
walnut *n*	**noix** *nf*
want *v*	**désirer** *v*
war *n*	**guerre** *nf*
wardrobe *n*	**armoire** *nf*
wash *v*	**laver** *v*
wasp *n*	**guêpe** *nf*
watch *n*	**montre** *nf*
water *n*	**eau** *nf*
water-colour *n*	**aquarelle** *nf*
wave *n*	**vague** *nf*
wealthy *adj*	**riche** *adj*
web *n*	**toile** *nf*
wedding *n*	**noce** *nf*
weed *n*	**mauvaise herbe** *nf*
weep *v*	**pleurer** *v*
weight-lifting *n*	**haltérophilie** *nf*
weird *adj*	**bizarre** *adj*
welcome *n*	**bienvenue** *nf*
wheat *n*	**blé** *nm*
wheel *n*	**roue** *nf*
whoever *pron*	**quiconque** *pron*

whole *adj*	**entier** *adj*
wholefoods *n pl*	**bio** (produits) *adj*
wicker *n*	**osier** *nm*
wide *adj*	**large** *adj*
wild *adj*	**sauvage** *adj*
win *v*	**gagner** *v*
window *n*	**fenêtre** *nf*
wine *n*	**vin** *nm*
wipe *v*	**essuyer** *v*
wish *v*	**souhaiter** *v*
with *prep*	**avec** *prép*
witness *n*	**témoin** *nm*
wood *n*	**bois** *nm*
wool *n*	**laine** *nf*
word *n*	**parole** *nf* **mot** *nm*
work *v*	**travailler** *v*
worker *n*	**ouvrier** *nm*
workshop *n*	**atelier** *nm*
world *n*	**monde** *nm*
wrinkle *n*	**ride** *nf*
wrist *n*	**poignet** *nm*
write *v*	**écrire** *v*
wrong *adj*	**faux** *adj*
wrong *n*	**tort** *nm*

Y

yesterday *adv*	**hier** *adv*
young *adj*	**jeune** *adj*

Z

zebra crossing *n*	**passage piétons** *nm*
zip fastener *n*	**fermeture éclair** *nf*

A

abîmer *v*	**damage** *v*
abri *nm*	**shelter** *n*
achats *nm pl*	**shopping** *n*
acheter *v*	**buy** *v*
adaptateur *nm*	**adaptor** *n*
addition (restaurant) *nf*	**bill** *n*
aéroport *nm*	**airport** *n*
affaires *nf pl*	**business** *n* **personal belongings** *n pl*
affiche *nf*	**poster** *n*
affreux *adj*	**awful** *adj*
âgé *adj*	**old** *adj* (person)
s'agenouiller *v*	**kneel down** *v*
agression *nf*	**mugging** *n*
aide *nf*	**help** *n*
aimable *adj*	**kind** *adj*
aimer *v*	**love** *v*
aller *v*	**go** *v*
allumer *v*	**light** *v* **switch on** *v*
allumettes *nf pl*	**matches** *n pl*
amarrer *v*	**moor** *v*
ambassade *nf*	**embassy** *n*
amende *nf*	**fine** *n*
amener *v*	**bring** *v*
amer *adj*	**bitter** *adj*
ami *nm*	**friend** *n*
amitié *nf*	**friendship** *n*
amour *nm*	**love** *n*
ampoule *nf*	**lightbulb** *n* **blister** *n*
s'amuser *v*	**enjoy** *v*
amygdales *nf pl*	**tonsils** *n*
analgésique *nm*	**pain-killer** *n*

anniversaire *nm*	**birthday** *n*
annuaire *nm*	**phone directory** *n*
annuler *v*	**cancel** *v*
antibiotique *nm*	**antibiotic** *n*
appareil photo *nm*	**camera** *n*
appeler *v*	**call** *v*
apprendre *v*	**learn** *v*
après *adv*	**after** *adv*
après-midi *nm*	**afternoon** *n*
aquarelle *nf*	**water-colour** *n*
araignée *nf*	**spider** *n*
arbre *nm*	**tree** *n*
argent *nm*	**money** *n* **silver** *n* (metal)
argent *adj*	**silver** *adj*
armoire *nf*	**wardrobe** *n* **cupboard** *n*
arrêter *v*	**stop** *v*
arrhes *nf pl*	**deposit** *n*
arrière *adv*	**behind** *adv*
arrivée *nf*	**arrival** *n*
artisanat *nm*	**handicrafts** *n pl*
ascenseur *nm*	**lift** *n*
s'asseoir *v*	**sit down** *v*
assez *adv*	**enough** *adv*
assurance *nf*	**insurance** *n*
atelier *nm*	**workshop** *n* **studio** *n*
attendre *v*	**wait** *v*
atterrissage *nm*	**landing** *n*
aujourd'hui *adv*	**today** *adv*
autostop *nm*	**hitchhiking** *n*
autre *adj*	**other** *adj* **another** *adj*
avaler *v*	**swallow** *v*
avant *adv*	**before** *adv*

125

avec *prép*	**with** *prep*
aveugle *adj*	**blind** *adj*
avion *nm*	**plane** *n*
avis *nm*	**opinion** *n*
avoine *nf*	**oats** *n pl*
avoir *v*	**have** *v*

B

bagages *nm pl*	**luggage** *n*
bagarre *nf*	**fight** *n*
bague *nf*	**ring** *n*
baignoire *nf*	**bathtub** *n*
bain *nm*	**bath** *n*
baiser *nm*	**kiss** *n*
baisser *v*	**lower** *v*
balcon *nm*	**balcony** *n*
ballon *nm*	**ball** *n*, **balloon** *n*
barbe *nf*	**beard** *n*
bateau *nm*	**boat** *n*
bâtiment *nm*	**building** *n*
beaucoup *adv*	**a lot** *adv*
besoin *nm*	**need** *n*
bête *nf*	**creature** *n*
bête *adj*	**silly** *adj* **stupid** *adj*
biberon *nm*	**bottle** *n* (baby's)
bibliothèque *nf*	**library** *n* **bookcase** *n*
bientôt *adv*	**soon** *adv*
bienvenue *nf*	**welcome** *n*
bijou *nm*	**gem** *n*, **piece of jewellery** *n*
billet *nm*	**ticket** *n*
bio (produits) *adj*	**wholefoods** *n pl*
bizarre *adj*	**weird** *adj*
blague *nf*	**joke** *n*

blé *nm*	**wheat** *n*
blessé *adj*	**injured** *adj*
blouson *nm*	**bomber jacket** *n*
bocal *nm*	**glass jar** *n*
boire *v*	**drink** *v*
bois *nm*	**wood** *n*
boisson *nf*	**drink** *n*
boîte *nf*	**box** *n*, **tin** *n*
boîte de nuit *nf*	**nightclub** *n*
bon *adj*	**good** *adj*
bon marché *adj*	**cheap** *adj*
bonbon *nm*	**sweet** *n*
bosse *nf*	**bump** *n*
bouche *nf*	**mouth** *n*
boucher *v*	**block** *v*
boussole *nf*	**compass** *n*
bout *nm*	**end** *n*
bouteille *nf*	**bottle** *n*
boutique *nf*	**shop** *n*
bouton *nm*	**spot** *n*, **button** *n*
bras *nm*	**arm** *n*
brique *nf*	**brick** *n*
briquet *nm*	**lighter** *n*
bronzer *v*	**sunbathe** *v*
brosse *nf*	**brush** *n*
brosse à dents *nf*	**toothbrush** *n*
bruit *nm*	**noise** *n*
brûler *v*	**burn** *v*
bruyant *adj*	**noisy** *adj*
bureau *nm*	**office** *n*
but *nm*	**goal** *n*

C

cacahuète *nf*	**peanut** *n*
cadeau *nm*	**gift** *n*
cadenas *nm*	**padlock** *n*

cafard *nm*	**cockroach** *n*	cheval *nm*	**horse** *n*
caillou *nm*	**pebble** *n*	cheveux *nm pl*	**hair** *n*
caisse *nf*	**cash desk** *n*	cheville *nf*	**ankle** *n*
calme *adj*	**quiet** *adj*	chèvre *nf*	**goat** *n*
camion *nm*	**lorry** *n*	chien *nm*	**dog** *n*
campagne *nf*	**countryside** *n*	chips *nf pl*	**potato crisps** *n pl*
canard *nm*	**duck** *n*	choc *nm*	**shock** *n*
carte (plan) *nf*	**map** *n*	choisir *v*	**choose** *v*
carte de crédit *nf*	**credit card** *n*	chose *nf*	**thing** *n*
		cil *nm*	**eyelash** *n*
casher *adj*	**kosher** *adj*	ciseaux *nm pl*	**scissors** *n pl*
casquette *nf*	**cap** *n*	clairière *nf*	**clearing** *n*
casser *v*	**break** *v*	clé *nf*	**key** *n*
caution *nf*	**deposit** *n*	clé anglaise *nf*	**wrench** *n*
célèbre *adj*	**famous** *adj*	climatisation *nf*	**air conditioning** *n*
célibataire *adj*	**single** *adj*		
cendrier *nm*	**ash tray** *n*	clochard *nm*	**tramp** *n*
centre-ville *nm*	**city centre** *n*	cloche *nf*	**bell** *n*
chair *nf*	**flesh** *n*	clou *nm*	**nail** *n*
chaise *nf*	**chair** *n*	cochon *nm*	**pig** *n*
chambre (à coucher) *nf*	**(bed)room** *n*	cœur *nm*	**heart** *n*
		coffre-fort *nm*	**safe** *n*
champ *nm*	**field** *n*	coiffeur *nm*	**hairdresser** *n*
changer *v*	**change** *v*	colère *nf*	**anger** *n*
chanson *nf*	**song** *n*	colis *nm*	**parcel** *n*
chanter *v*	**sing** *v*	colle *nf*	**glue** *n*
chapeau *nm*	**hat** *n*	colline *nf*	**hill** *n*
charbon *nm*	**coal** *n*	colonne vertébrale *nf*	**spine** *n* **backbone** *n*
chat *nm*	**cat** *n*		
chaud *adj*	**hot** *adj*	commander (restaurant) *v*	**order** *v*
chaussette *nf*	**sock** *n*		
chaussures *nf pl*	**shoes** *n pl*	commencer *v*	**start** *v*
chef-d'œuvre *nm*	**masterpiece** *n*	complet *adj*	**full** *adj*
cheminée *nf*	**fireplace** *n*	comprendre *v*	**understand** *v*
chemise *nf*	**shirt** *n*	compris *adj*	**included** *adj*
chemisier *nm*	**blouse** *n*	concert *nm*	**concert** *n*
cher *adj*	**expensive** *adj*	conduire *v*	**drive** *v*, **lead** *v*
chercher *v*	**look for** *v*	confiture *nf*	**jam** *n*

127

connaître v	know v (someone)
conseil nm	advice n
consigne nf	left-luggage office n
consulat nm	consulate n
contraire nm	opposite n
contre prép	against prep
coq nm	cock n
cou nm	neck n
couches-culottes nf pl	disposable nappies n pl
coude nm	elbow n
couler v	run v
couloir nm	corridor n
couper v	cut v
cour nf	courtyard n
courir v	run v
courrier nm	mail n
court adj	short adj
coussin nm	cushion n
couteau nm	knife n
coûter v	cost v
crâne nm	skull n
crayon nm	pencil n
crème nf	cream n
crier v	shout v
croire v	believe v
cuiller nf	spoon n
cuisine nf	kitchen n
cuisse nf	thigh n

D

dangereux adj	dangerous adj
dé nm	dice n
dé à coudre nm	thimble n
déambuler v	stroll v
debout adv	standing adj
débutant nm	beginner n
déchirer v	tear v
décollage nm	take-off n
décompresser v	relax v
découvrir v	discover v
déçu adj	disappointed adj
défilé nm	parade n
dégâts nm pl	damage n
dégoût nm	disgust n
déguster v	taste v, sample v
dehors adv	outside adv
déjeuner nm	lunch n
délabré adj	run-down adj
demain adv	tomorrow adv
demander v	ask v
démanger v	itch v
démarrer v	start v
demi-pension nf	half board n
dent nf	tooth n
dentifrice nm	toothpaste n
dentiste nm	dentist n
dépanneuse nf	breakdown truck n
départ nm	departure n
dépenser v	spend v
depuis prép	since prep
déranger v	disturb v
dernier adj	last adj
derrière adv	behind adv
désastre nm	disaster n
désinfectant nm	disinfectant n
désolé adj	sorry adj
désossé adj	boned adj
dessert nm	dessert n
dessin nm	drawing n
dessin animé nm	cartoon n
dessous prép	beneath prep

dessus *prép*	**on top of** *prep*
détester *v*	**hate** *v*
dévaliser *v*	**raid** *v*
devant *prép*	**in front of** *prep*
devenir *v*	**become** *v*
devises *nf pl*	**currency** *n*
devoir *v*	**owe** *v*
	have to *v*
difficile *adj*	**difficult** *adj*
dîner *nm*	**dinner** *n*
dire *v*	**say** *v*
disparaître *v*	**disappear** *v*
disponible *adj*	**available** *adj*
disque *nm*	**record** *n*
distributeur automatique *nm*	**cash machine** *n*
divorcé *adj*	**divorced** *adj*
doigt *nm*	**finger** *n*
dommage! *nm*	**what a pity!** *loc*
dommages *nm pl*	**damage** *n*
donner *v*	**give** *v*
dormir *v*	**sleep** *v*
dos *nm*	**back** *n*
douane *nf*	**customs** *n pl*
douche *nf*	**shower** *n*
douleur *nf*	**pain** *n*
doux *adj*	**sweet** *adj*
	gentle *adj*
drap *nm*	**sheet** *n*
drapeau *nm*	**flag** *n*
droit *adj*	**straight** *adj*
à droite *loc*	**on the right** *loc*
de droite *loc*	**right-wing** *adj*
droit *nm*	**right** *n*, **law** *n*
droitier *adj*	**right-handed** *adj*
drôle *adj*	**funny** *adj*
dur *adj*	**hard** *adj*

E

eau *nf*	**water** *n*
écharpe *nf*	**scarf** *n*
échec *nm*	**failure** *n*
échecs *nm pl*	**chess** *n*
échelle *nf*	**ladder** *n*
école *nf*	**school** *n*
écouter *v*	**listen** *v*
écrire *v*	**write** *v*
efficace *adj*	**efficient** *adj*
égoût *nm*	**sewer** *n*
égratignure *nf*	**scratch** *n*
embouteillage *nm*	**traffic jam** *n*
embrasser *v*	**kiss** *v*
émission *nf*	**radio/TV programme** *n*
emmener *v*	**take** *v*
emporter *v*	**take away** *v*
emprunter *v*	**borrow** *v*
enceinte *adj*	**pregnant** *adj*
enceinte *nf*	**boundary** *n*
encre *nf*	**ink** *n*
enfant *nm*	**child** *n*
enfer *nm*	**hell** *n*
ennuyeux *adj*	**boring** *adj*
entendre *v*	**hear** *v*
entier *adj*	**whole** *adj*
entorse *nf*	**sprain** *n*
environ *adv*	**about** *adv*
envoyer *v*	**send** *v*
épaule *nf*	**shoulder** *n*
épicerie *nf*	**grocery** *n*
épingle *nf*	**pin** *n*
épingle de nourrice *nf*	**safety pin** *n*
épouser *v*	**marry** *v*

French	English
épuisé *adj*	**exhausted** *adj* **out of print/stock**
équipe *nf*	**team** *n*
erreur *nf*	**mistake** *n*
escalier *nm*	**staircase** *n*
escargot *nm*	**snail** *n*
espoir *nm*	**hope** *n*
essayer *v*	**try** *v*
essence *nf*	**petrol** *n*
esseulé *adj*	**lonely** *adj*
essuyer *v*	**wipe** *v*
étang *nm*	**pool** *n*
éternuer *v*	**sneeze** *v*
étiquette *nf*	**label** *n*
étoile *nf*	**star** *n*
étrange *adj*	**strange** *adj*
étranger *nm*	**foreigner** *n*
étriqué *adj*	**skimpy** *adj*
étroit *adj*	**narrow** *adj*
étudiant *nm*	**student** *n*
exposition *nf*	**exhibition** *n*
exprès *adv*	**on purpose** *adv*

F

fâché *adj*	**angry** *adj*
facteur *nm*	**postman** *n*
facture *nf*	**invoice** *n*
faim *nf*	**hunger** *n*
faire *v*	**do** *v*, **make** *v*
falaise *nf*	**cliff** *n*
famille *nf*	**family** *n*
fantôme *nm*	**ghost** *n*
fatigué *adj*	**tired** *adj*
faune *nf*	**fauna** *n*
fauteuil *nm*	**armchair** *n*
félicitations! *nf pl*	**congratulations!** *n pl*

French	English
fenêtre *nf*	**window** *n*
ferme *nf*	**farm** *n*
ferme *adj*	**solid** *adj* **strong** *adj*
fermer *v*	**close** *v*
fermeture éclair *nf*	**zip** *n*
fesse *nf*	**buttock** *n*
feu *nm*	**fire** *n* **traffic light** *n*
feuilleton *nm*	**serial** *n*
ficelle *nf*	**string** *n*
figure *nf*	**face** *n*
fil dentaire *nm*	**dental floss** *n*
filtre *nm*	**filter** *n*
flèche *nf*	**arrow** *n*
fleur *nf*	**flower** *n*
fleuve *nm*	**river** *n*
flirter *v*	**flirt** *v*
flore *nf*	**flora** *n*
foi *nf*	**faith** *n*
foie *nm*	**liver** *n*
fondre *v*	**melt** *v*
force *nf*	**strength** *n*
forêt *nf*	**forest** *n*
formulaire *nm*	**form** *n*
fort *adj*	**strong** *adj*
fou *adj*	**mad** *adj* **crazy** *adj*
fouler *v*	**sprain** *v*
frapper *v*	**hit** *v*
frites *nf pl*	**chips** *n pl*
froid *adj*	**cold** *adj*
fromage *nm*	**cheese** *n*
front *nm*	**forehead** *n*
fumée *nf*	**smoke** *n*
fumer *v*	**smoke** *v*
fusain *nm*	**charcoal** *n*

G

gagner *v*	**earn** *v*, **win** *v*
galet *nm*	**pebble** *n*
gant *nm*	**glove** *n*
gant de toilette *nm*	**face cloth** *n*
garder *v*	**keep** *v*
gare *nf*	**station** *n*
garer *v*	**park** *n*
gâter *v*	**spoil** *v*
gauche *adj*	**left** *adj*
à gauche *loc*	**on the left** *loc*
de gauche *loc*	**left-wing** *adj*
gaucher *adj*	**left-handed** *adj*
gazon *nm*	**lawn** *n*
geler *v*	**freeze** *v*
gêner *v*	**trouble** *v* **embarras** *v*
généreux *adj*	**generous** *adj*
genou *nm*	**knee** *n*
gentil *adj*	**nice** *adj*, **kind** *adj*
gérant *nm*	**manager** *n*
glace *nf*	**ice** *n*, **ice cream** *n*
glacière *nf*	**icebox** *n*
glaçon *nm*	**ice cube** *n*
gloire *nf*	**fame** *n*, **glory** *n*
gomme *nf*	**eraser** *n*
gorge *nf*	**throat** *n*
goût *nm*	**taste** *n*
goûter *nm*	**afternoon snack** *n*
goûter *v*	**taste** *v*
goutte *nf*	**drop** *n*
graine *nf*	**seed** *n*
grand *adj*	**big** *adj*
grange *nf*	**barn** *n*
gratter *v*	**scratch** *v*

gratuit *adj*	**free** *adj*
grave *adj*	**serious** *adj*
grippe *nf*	**flu** *n*
gros *adj*	**fat** *adj*
grossier *adj*	**rude** *adj* **coarse** *adj*
guêpe *nf*	**wasp** *n*
guerre *nf*	**war** *n*
gueule de bois *nf*	**hangover** *n*
guichet *nm*	**ticket office** *n*
guidon *nm*	**handlebars** *n pl*

H

habile *adj*	**clever** *adj* **dexterous** *adj*
habillé *adj*	**dressed** *adj* **clothed** *adj*
habit *nm*	**clothing** *n*
habitant *nm*	**inhabitant** *n*
habiter *v*	**live in** *v*
habitude *nf*	**habit** *n*
d'habitude *loc*	**usually** *adv*
hache *nf*	**axe** *n*
hachoir *nm*	**chopper** *n* **mincer** *n*
haie *nf*	**hedge** *n*
haine *nf*	**hatred** *n*
haïr *v*	**hate** *v*
hameçon *nm*	**fishhook** *n*
hanche *nf*	**hip** *n*
handicapé *adj*	**disabled** *adj*
haras *nm*	**stud farm** *n*
harceler *v*	**harass** *v*
haricot *nm*	**bean** *n*
hasard *nm*	**chance** *n*
hâte *nf*	**haste** *n*

hausse *nf* — **rise** *n*
hautain *adj* — **haughty** *adj*
hébergement *nm* — **accommodation** *n*
hébété *adj* — **dazed** *adj*
herbe *nf* — **grass** *n*
hibou *nm* — **owl** *n*
hier *adv* — **yesterday** *adv*
histoire *nf* — **story** *n*, **history** *n*
hommage *nm* — **tribute** *n*
homme d'affaires *nm* — **businessman** *n*
honoraires *nm pl* — **fees** *n pl*
honte *nf* — **shame** *n*
hoquet *nm* — **hiccoughs** *n pl*
horaire *nm* — **timetable** *n*
horloge *nf* — **clock** *n*
horreur *nf* — **horror** *n*
horrifié *adj* — **horrified** *adj*
huile *nf* — **oil** *n*
humide *adj* — **damp** *adj*

I

ici *adv* — **here** *adv*
idée *nf* — **idea** *n*
identité *nf* — **identity** *n*
île *nf* — **island** *n*
illustrer *v* — **illustrate** *v*
immortel *adj* — **immortal** *adj*
imperméable *nm* — **raincoat** *n*
impôt *nm* — **tax** *n*
imprimante *nf* — **printer** *n*
imprimeur *nm* — **printer** *n*
incendie *nm* — **fire** *n*
inconfortable *adj* — **uncomfortable** *adj*
incroyable *adj* — **unbelievable** *adj*

indéterminé *adj* — **undetermined** *adj*
indiquer *v* — **show** *v*
indisposé *adj* — **upset** *adj*, **annoyed** *adj*
infect *adj* — **disgusting** *adj*
infini *adj* — **infinite** *adj*
infirmière *nf* — **nurse** *n*
infortune *nf* — **misfortune** *n*
ingénieur *nm* — **engineer** *n*
inouï *adj* — **unheard of** *adj*
s'inquiéter *v* — **worry** *v*
inscrire *v* — **write down** *v*
s'inscrire *v* — **sign on** *v*
insecte *nm* — **insect** *n*
insolation *nf* — **sunstroke** *n*
insulaire *adj* — **insular** *adj*
intéressant *adj* — **interesting** *adj*
intermittent *nm* — **casual worker** *n*
interrupteur *nm* — **electric switch** *n*
intime *adj* — **intimate** *adj*
isolant *adj* — **insulating** *adj*
isolé *adj* — **isolated** *adj*
itinéraire *nm* — **route** *n*
ivre *adj* — **drunk** *adj*
ivrogne *nm* — **drunkard** *n*

J

jaloux *adj* — **jealous** *adj*
jamais *adv* — **never** *adv*
jambe *nf* — **leg** *n*
jambon *nm* — **ham** *n*
jante *nf* — **rim** *n*
jardin *nm* — **garden** *n*
jauge *nf* — **gauge** *n*
jeter *v* — **throw** *v*
jeu *nm* — **game** *n*

French	English
jeune *adj*	**young** *adj*
joindre *v*	**join** *v*
joli *adj*	**pretty** *adj*
joue *nf*	**cheek** *n*
jouer *v*	**play** *v*
jouet *nm*	**toy** *n*
jour *nm*	**day** *n*
journal *nm*	**newspaper** *n*
journal intime *nm*	**diary** *n*
journalier *adj*	**daily** *adj*
jumelles *nf pl*	**binoculars** *n pl*
jupe *nf*	**skirt** *n*
jus *nm*	**juice** *n*
jusqu'à *prép*	**until** *prep*
juste *adj*	**correct** *adj*
justice *nf*	**law** *n*, **justice** *n*
juteux *adj*	**juicy** *adj*

K

kilométrage *nm*	**mileage** *n*
kinésithérapeute *nm*	**physiotherapist** *n*
kiosque *nm*	**kiosk** *n*
klaxon *nm*	**horn** *n* (car)

L

lac *nm*	**lake** *n*
lacet *nm*	**shoelace** *n*
laid *adj*	**ugly** *adj*
laine *nf*	**wool** *n*
laisser *v*	**leave** *v*
lait *nm*	**milk** *n*
lame *nf*	**blade** *n*
lampe *nf*	**lamp** *n*
lancer *v*	**throw** *v*
lande *nf*	**moor** *n*
langue *nf*	**tongue** *n* **language** *n*
lapin *nm*	**rabbit** *n*
laque *nf*	**lacquer** *n* **hair spray** *n*
large *adj*	**wide** *adj*
larme *nf*	**tear** *n*
laver *v*	**wash** *v*
lèche-vitrine *nm*	**window-shopping** *n*
légume *nm*	**vegetable** *n*
lent *adj*	**slow** *adj*
lentille *nf*	**lens** *n*
lentilles *nf pl*	**lentils** *n pl*
lessive *nf*	**laundry** *n* **washing powder** *n*
lèvre *nf*	**lip** *n*
liberté *nf*	**freedom** *n*
librairie *nf*	**bookshop** *n*
libre *adj*	**free** *adj*
liquide *nm*	**liquid** *n*
lire *v*	**read** *v*
lit *nm*	**bed** *n*
livre *nf*	**pound** *n*
livre *nm*	**book** *n*
logement *nm*	**lodgings** *n pl* **accommodation** *n*
logiciel *nm*	**software** *n*
loin *adv*	**far** *adv*
loisirs *nm pl*	**leisure activities** *n pl*
longueur *nf*	**length** *n*
louer *v*	**hire** *v*
loup *nm*	**wolf** *n*
loupe *nf*	**magnifying glass** *n*

lourd *adj*	**heavy** *adj*
loyer *nm*	**rent** *n*
lumière *nf*	**light** *n*
lune *nf*	**moon** *n*
lune de miel *nf*	**honeymoon** *n*

M

machine à laver *nf*	**washing machine** *n*
magasin *nm*	**shop** *n*
maillot de bain *nm*	**bathing costume** *n*
main *nf*	**hand** *n*
maintenant *adv*	**now** *adv*
mais *conj*	**but** *conj*
maison *nf*	**house** *n*
maître-nageur *nm*	**lifeguard** *n*
malade *adj*	**ill** *adj*
malentendu *nm*	**misunderstanding** *n*
manger *v*	**eat** *v*
manifestation *nf*	**demonstration** *n*
manquer *v*	**miss** *v*
manteau *nm*	**coat** *n*
marché *nm*	**market** *n*
marié *adj*	**married** *adj*
marrant *adj*	**funny** *adj*
marteau *nm*	**hammer** *n*
matériel *nm*	**equipment** *n*
médecin *nm*	**doctor** *n*
menton *nm*	**chin** *n*
mer *nf*	**sea** *n*
messe *nf*	**mass** *n*
métro *nm*	**underground** *n*
meuble *nm*	**piece of furniture** *n*

miette *nf*	**crumb** *n*
mieux *adv, adj*	**better** *adv, adj*
miroir *nm*	**mirror** *n*
moine *nm*	**monk** *n*
moineau *nm*	**sparrow** *n*
moisi *adj*	**mouldy** *adj*
mollet *nm*	**shin** *n*
monde *nm*	**world** *n*
monnaie *nf*	**change** *n*
montagne *nf*	**mountain** *n*
montre *nf*	**watch** *n*
montrer *v*	**show** *v*
morceau *nm*	**piece** *n*
mou *adj*	**soft** *adj*
mouche *nf*	**fly** *n*
mouchoir *nm*	**handkerchief** *n*
moule *nf*	**mussel** *n*
moustique *nm*	**mosquito** *n*
mouton *nm*	**sheep** *n*
mur *nm*	**wall** *n*
mûr *adj*	**ripe** *adj*
muscle *nm*	**muscle** *n*
musique *nf*	**music** *n*
myope *adj*	**short-sighted** *adj*

N

nager *v*	**swim** *v*
naître *v*	**be born** *v*
nappe *nf*	**tablecloth** *n*
narguer *v*	**scoff at** *v*
narine *nf*	**nostril** *n*
natation *nf*	**swimming** *n*
natif *adj*	**native** *adj*
naufrage *nm*	**shipwreck** *n*
néant *nm*	**nothingness** *n*
nécessaire *adj*	**necessary** *adj*
négliger *v*	**neglect** *v*

neige *nf*	**snow** *n*
nerf *nm*	**nerve** *n*
nerveux *adj*	**nervous** *adj*
net *adj*	**clean** *adj*
	neat *adj*
nettoyer *v*	**clean** *v*
neuf *adj*	**new** *adj*
neutre *adj*	**neutral** *adj*
nez *nm*	**nose** *n*
niche *nf*	**recess** *n*
	kennel *n*
nid *nm*	**nest** *n*
nier *v*	**deny** *v*
niveau *nm*	**level** *n*
noce *nf*	**wedding** *n*
nocif *adj*	**noxious** *adj*
	harmful *adj*
nœud *nm*	**knot** *n*
noisette *nf*	**hazelnut** *n*
noix *nf*	**walnut** *n*
nombre *nm*	**number** *n*
nombreux *adj*	**numerous** *adj*
nombril *nm*	**navel** *n*
nonne *nf*	**nun** *n*
nouer *v*	**tie** *v*, **knot** *v*
nouilles *nf pl*	**noodles** *n pl*
nounours *nm*	**teddy bear** *n*
nourriture *nf*	**food** *n*
nouveau *adj*	**new** *adj*
nouvelles *nf pl*	**news** *n pl*
noyau *nm*	**core** *n*, **kernel** *n*
noyer *v*	**drown** *v*
nu *nm*	**nude** *n*
nu *adj*	**naked** *adj*
nuage *nm*	**cloud** *n*
nuire *v*	**harm** *v*
nuit *nf*	**night** *n*
numéro *nm*	**number** *n*

O

obéir *v*	**obey** *v*
obligatoire *adj*	**compulsory** *adj*
occident *nm*	**west** *n*
occupé *adj*	**engaged** *adj*
	busy *adj*
odeur *nf*	**smell** *n*
œil *nm*	**eye** *n*
œuf *nm*	**egg** *n*
œuf dur *nm*	**hard-boiled egg** *n*
œuf mollet *nm*	**soft-boiled egg** *n*
offrir *v*	**give** *v*
oiseau *nm*	**bird** *n*
ombre *nf*	**shade** *n*
	shadow *n*
ombrelle *nf*	**paralol** *n*
ondée *nf*	**shower of rain** *n*
ongle *nm*	**nail** *n*
opportun *adj*	**timely** *adj*
or *nm*	**gold** *n*
ordinateur *nm*	**computer** *n*
ordures *nf pl*	**rubbish** *n*
oreille *nf*	**ear** *n*
oreillons *nm pl*	**mumps** *n pl*
orfèvre *nm*	**goldsmith** *n*
orgueil *nm*	**pride** *n*
orient *nm*	**east** *n*
orner *v*	**decorate** *v*
orteil *nm*	**toe** *n*
os *nm*	**bone** *n*
oseille *nf*	**sorrel** *n*
oser *v*	**dare** *v*
osier *nm*	**wicker** *v*
ôter *v*	**take off** *v*
ouate *nf*	**cotton wool** *n*

135

oublier *v*	**forget** *v*	peur *nf*	**fear** *n*
ouragan *nm*	**hurricane** *n*	peut-être *adv*	**perhaps** *adv*
ourlet *nm*	**hem** *n*	photo *nf*	**picture** *n*
ours *nm*	**bear** *n*	pied *nm*	**foot** *n*
outil *nm*	**tool** *n*	pierre *nf*	**stone** *n*
outre *prép*	**as well as** *adv*	piéton *nm*	**pedestrian** *n*
outré *adj*	**outraged** *adj*	pile *nf*	**battery** *n*
ouvre-boîte *nm*	**tin opener** *n*	pipe *nf*	**pipe** *n*
ouvreuse *nf*	**usherette** *n*	piqûre *nf*	**injection** *n*
ouvrier *nm*	**worker** *n*		**insect bite** *n*
ouvrir *v*	**open** *v*	piscine *nf*	**swimming pool** *n*
		piste *nf*	**track** *n*

P

		placard *nm*	**cupboard** *n*
		plafond *nm*	**ceiling** *n*
pain *nm*	**bread** *n*	plage *nf*	**beach** *n*
paix *nf*	**peace** *n*	plaisanterie *nf*	**joke** *n*
palmier *nm*	**palm tree** *n*	plan *nm*	**town map** *n*
papier *nm*	**paper** *n*	plancher *nm*	**floor** *n*
papilles *nf pl*	**tastebuds** *n pl*	plante *nf*	**plant** *n*
papillon *nm*	**butterfly** *n*	plateau *nm*	**tray** *n*
paradis *nm*	**paradise** *n*	plein *adj*	**full** *adj*
parapluie *nm*	**umbrella** *n*	pleurer *v*	**cry** *v*, **weep** *v*
paresseux *adj*	**lazy** *adj*	plumeau *nm*	**feather duster** *n*
parler *v*	**speak** *v*	poêle *nf*	**frying pan** *n*
parole *nf*	**word** *n*	poêle *nm*	**stove** *n*
partager *v*	**share** *v*	poème *nm*	**poem** *n*
partir *v*	**leave** *v*, **go** *v*	poignet *nm*	**wrist** *n*
pâtes *nf pl*	**pasta** *n*	poil *nm*	**hair** *n*
payer *v*	**pay** *v*	poitrine *nf*	**chest** *n*
paysage *nm*	**landscape** *n*	porte *nf*	**door** *n*
paupière *nf*	**eyelid** *n*	portefeuille *nm*	**wallet** *n*
pauvre *adj*	**poor** *adj*	pouce *nm*	**thumb** *n*
peau *nf*	**skin** *n*	poule *nf*	**hen** *n*
perdre *v*	**loose** *v*	poulet *nm*	**chicken** *n*
permettre *v*	**allow** *v*	poumon *nm*	**lung** *n*
petit-déjeuner *nm*	**breakfast** *n*	poupée *nf*	**doll** *n*
		pourboire *nm*	**tip** *n*
peu *adv*	**a little** *adv*	pouvoir *nm*	**power** *n*

pouvoir *v*	**be able** *v*
pré *nm*	**meadow** *n*
premier *adj*	**first** *adj*
prendre *v*	**take** *v*
près *adv*	**near** *adv*
presbyte *adj*	**long-sighted** *adj*
préservatif *nm*	**condom** *n*
prochain *adj*	**next** *adj*
profession *nf*	**job** *n*
propre *adj*	**clean** *adj*
publicité *nf*	**advertisement** *n*

Q

quai *nm*	**platform** *n*
	quay *n*
quantité *nf*	**amount** *n*
quartier *nm*	**district** *n*
quasi *adv*	**almost** *adv*
quatre-quatre (4x4) *nm*	**four-wheel-drive vehicle** *n*
quelqu'un *pron*	**someone** *pron*
quelque chose *loc ind*	**something** *pron*
quelquefois *adv*	**sometimes** *adv*
querelle *nf*	**quarrel** *n*
question *nf*	**question** *n*
queue *nf* (animal)	**queue** *n* **tail** *n*
quiconque *pron*	**whoever** *pron*
quilles (jeu) *nf pl*	**skittles** *n pl*
quincaillerie *nf*	**ironmongers** *n* **hardware shop** *n*
quinte de toux *nf*	**fit of coughing** *n*
quinzaine *nf*	**fortnight** *n*
quitter *v*	**leave** *v*
quotidien *adj*	**daily** *adj*

R

rabais *nm*	**reduction** *n*
raccourcir *v*	**shorten** *v*
raconter *v*	**tell** *v* (story)
raide *adj*	**stiff** *adj*
raison *nf*	**reason** *n*
avoir raison *v*	**be right** *v*
randonnée *nf*	**hiking** *n*
rang *nm*	**row** *n*
ranger *v*	**tidy up** *v*
réalisateur *nm*	**film director** *n*
recevoir *v*	**receive** *v*
réchaud *nm*	**heater** *n* **primus stove** *n*
reconnaître *v*	**recognise** *v*
reçu *nm*	**receipt** *n*
recyclage *nm*	**recycling** *n*
regarder *v*	**look at** *v*
régime *nm*	**diet** *n*
rein *nm*	**kidney** *n*
reine *nf*	**queen** *n*
renard *nm*	**fox** *n*
rendez-vous *nm*	**appointment** *n*
rendre *v*	**give back** *v*
renseignement *nm*	**information** *n*
réparer *v*	**repair** *v*
repas *nm*	**meal** *n*
repassage *nm*	**ironing** *n*
repos *nm*	**rest** *n*
réserver *v*	**book** *v*
respirer *v*	**breathe** *v*
rester *v*	**stay** *v*
retard *nm*	**delay** *n*
retourner *v*	**go back** *v* **return** *v*
réveil *nm*	**alarm clock** *n*

réveiller *v*	**wake up** *v*
revenu *nm*	**income** *n*
rez-de-chaussée *nm*	**ground floor** *n*
rhume des foins *nm*	**hayfever** *n*
riche *adj*	**rich** *adj* **wealthy** *adj*
rideau *nm*	**curtain** *n*
rien *pron ind*	**nothing** *pron*
rire *v, nm*	**laugh** *v, n*
ristourne *nf*	**refund** *n*
riverain *nm*	**resident** *n*
rivière *nf*	**river** *n*
riz *nm*	**rice** *n*
robe *nf*	**dress** *n*
rocher *nm*	**rock** *n*
roi *nm*	**king** *n*
roman *nm*	**novel** *n*
rond *adj*	**round** *adj*
roue *nf*	**wheel** *n*
rouler *v*	**roll** *v*, **drive** *v*
rouler à droite	**drive on the right**
rue *nf*	**street** *n*

S

sable *nm*	**sand** *n*
sac *nm*	**bag** *n*
sac à dos *nm*	**rucksack** *n*
sac à main *nm*	**handbag** *n*
saigner *v*	**bleed** *v*
sale *adj*	**dirty** *adj*
salé *adj*	**salty** *adj*
salle à manger *nf*	**dining room** *n*
salle de bains *nf*	**bathroom** *n*
salon *nm*	**living room** *n*

saluer *v*	**greet** *v*
sang *nm*	**blood** *n*
saoul *adj*	**drunk** *adj*
sauf *prép*	**except** *prep*
sauvage *adj*	**wild** *adj* **timid** *adj*
savoir *v*	**know** *v* (something)
savon *nm*	**soap** *n*
séance *nf*	**performance** *n*
seau *nm*	**bucket** *n*
sécher *v*	**dry** *v*
secours *nm*	**help** *n*
sein *nm*	**breast** *n*
séjour *nm*	**stay** *v*
sel *nm*	**salt** *n*
semelle *nf*	**sole** *n*
sens *nm*	**sense** *n* **direction** *n*
sentiment *nm*	**feeling** *n*
sentir *v*	**smell** *v*
serpent *nm*	**snake** *n*
seuil *nm*	**threshold** *n*
seul *adj*	**alone** *adj* **lonely** *adj*
seulement *adv*	**only** *adv*
siège *nm*	**seat** *n*
singe *nm*	**monkey** *n*
soif *nf*	**thirst** *n*
soleil *nm*	**sun** *n*
sommeil *nm*	**sleep** *n*
sonner *v*	**ring** *v*
sonnette *nf*	**doorbell** *n*
souffler *v*	**blow** *v*
souhaiter *v*	**wish** *v*
sourcil *nm*	**eyebrow** *n*
sourd *adj*	**deaf** *adj*
sourire *v, nm*	**smile** *v, n*

souris *nf*	**mouse** *n*
souvent *adv*	**often** *adv*
se souvenir *v*	**remember** *v*
spectacle *nm*	**show** *n*
stylo *nm*	**pen** *n*
sucré *adj*	**sweet** *adj*
suivre *v*	**follow** *v*
supplémentaire *adj*	**extra** *adj*
survie *nf*	**survival** *n*
survivre *v*	**survive** *v*

T

table *nf*	**table** *n*
tableau *nm*	**picture** *n* **painting** *n*
taille *nf*	**size** *n*
tapis *nm*	**carpet** *n*
tard *adv*	**late** *adj*
tarif *nm*	**rate** *n*
téléphone portable *nm*	**mobile phone** *n*
témoin *nm*	**witness** *n*
tendre *adj*	**soft** *adj* **tender** *adj*
terrain *nm*	**plot of land** *n*
terrain de foot *nm*	**football ground** *n*
terre *nf*	**earth** *n*
tête *nf*	**head** *n*
thé *nm*	**tea** *n*
tiède *adj*	**lukewarm** *adj*
timbre *nm*	**stamp** *n*
tire-bouchon *nm*	**corkscrew** *n*
toile *nf*	**web** *n*, **cloth** *n*
toilettes *nf pl*	**toilets** *n pl*
toit *nm*	**roof** *n*

tort *nm*	**wrong** *n*
torticolis *nm*	**stiff neck** *n*
tortue *nf*	**tortoise** *n*
tôt *adv*	**early** *adv*
toucher *v*	**touch** *v*
toujours *adv*	**always** *adv*
tourne-vis *nm*	**screwdriver** *n*
tousser *v*	**cough** *v*
tout le monde *loc pron*	**everyone** *pron*
tout-terrain *nm* (vélo)	**mountain bike** *n*
traduire *v*	**translate** *v*
traiteur *nm*	**deli** *n*
travail *nm*	**job** *n*
travailler *v*	**work** *v*
traverser *v*	**cross** *v*
trop *adv*	**too much** *adv*
trottoir *nm*	**pavement** *n*
trou *nm*	**hole** *n*
trouvaille *nf*	**find** *n*
trouver *v*	**find** *v*
tuile *nf*	**tile** *n*

U

ultérieur *adj*	**later** *adj*
ultime *adj*	**last** *adj*, **final** *adj*
uni *adj*	**plain** *adj*
unir *v*	**unite** *v*
univers *nm*	**universe** *n*
urgence *nf*	**emergency** *n*
urinoir *nm*	**urinal** *n*
us et coutumes *nm pl, nf pl*	**customs** *n pl* **traditions** *n pl*
usé *adj*	**worn out** *adj*
usine *nf*	**factory** *n*
ustensile *nm*	**implement** *n*

French	English
usuel *adj*	**everyday** *adj* **ordinary** *adj*
utile *adj*	**useful** *adj*
utiliser *v*	**use** *v*

V

vacances *nf pl*	**holidays** *n pl*
vache *nf*	**cow** *n*
vague *nf*	**wave** *n*
vaincre *v*	**defeat** *v*
vaisselle *nf*	**crockery** *n*
faire la vaisselle *v*	**do the washing up** *v*
valider *v*	**validate** *v*
valise *nf*	**suitcase** *n*
varicelle *nf*	**chickenpox** *n*
veau *nm*	**calf** *n*, **veal** *n*
vedette *nf*	**movie star** *n*
végétarien *adj*	**vegetarian** *adj*
veille *nf*	**the day before** *n*
veiller *v*	**watch over** *v*
veilleur de nuit *nm*	**night watchman** *n*
vélo *nm*	**bicycle** *n*, **bike** *n*
velouté *adj*	**smooth** *adj*
vendanges *nf pl*	**grape harvest** *n*
vendre *v*	**sell** *v*
venir *v*	**come** *v*
ventre *nm*	**stomach** *n*
vérité *nf*	**truth** *n*
verre *nm*	**glass** *n*
verrouiller *v*	**bolt** *v*, **lock** *v*
vertigineux *adj*	**dizzying** *adj*
vessie *nf*	**bladder** *n*
veste *nf*	**jacket** *n*
vestiaire *nm*	**cloakroom** *n*
viande *nf*	**meat** *n*

French	English
vieux *adj*	**old** *adj*
vide *adj*	**empty** *adj*
vignoble *nm*	**vineyard** *n*
ville *nf*	**town** *n*
vin *nm*	**wine** *n*
viol *nm*	**rape** *n*
visage *nm*	**face** *n*
visiter *v*	**visit** *v*
vitre *nf*	**pane of glass** *v*
vitrine *nf*	**showcase** *n*
vivre *v*	**live** *v*
vœu *nm*	**wish** *n*
voilier *nm*	**sailing boat** *n*
voir *v*	**see** *v*
voiture *nf*	**car** *n*
voix *nf*	**voice** *n*
vol *nm*	**flight** *n* **theft** *n*
volaille *nf*	**poultry** *n*
volet *nm*	**shutter** *n*
voleur *nm*	**thief** *n*
vouloir *v*	**want** *v*
voyager *v*	**travel** *v*
vue *nf*	**view** *n* **eyesight** *n*

Y

y *adv*	**there** *adv*
yaourt *nm*	**yoghurt** *n*
yeux *nm pl*	**eyes** *n pl*

Z

zèbre *nm*	**zebra** *n*
zèle *nm*	**zeal** *n*
zeste de citron *nm*	**lemon peel** *n*